fierce
warrioress

Recognizing the Spiritual Battlefield and Learning to Fight

Jennifer Johnson

randall house
114 Bush Rd | Nashville, TN 37217 | randallhouse.com

Published by Randall House Publications
114 Bush Road
Nashville, TN 37217

Printed in the United States of America

ISBN 978-0-89265-786-5

Dedicated to Cynthia Huffmyer, Cynthia Jines,
Diane Spencer, Cheryl Herndon,
and Sky Merryman.
Thank you for fighting for and with me.

CONTENTS

Introduction 1

PART 1: DON'T BE AFRAID
    Week 1 6
    Week 2 33

PART 2: REMEMBER THE LORD
    Week 3 60
    Week 4 89

PART 3: AND FIGHT
    Week 5 120
    Week 6 151

Endnotes 184

My Spiritual Battle Plan 186

INTRODUCTION

We protect ourselves from "bad guys." We prepare. We plan. We prioritize. We don't talk to strangers. We don't go out late at night. We have alarm systems for our homes and cars. We have guard dogs. We pray for safety. We turn on our porch lights. We have neighbors get our mail and newspapers when we are out of town so that it gives the appearance we are home. We put a timer on an indoor lamp to come on when we are gone. We leave on the TV even when we've left the house for just an hour or two. We don't give our Social Security number to just anyone. We protect against identity theft. We don't let our children walk wherever they want. We even use devices such as child leashes just so our children don't leave our sight. This is just a small list of actions we take to protect what we value most.

In the spiritual realm, we have an enemy who has even developed plans for our lives. We may not be thinking about him, but rest assured, our enemy has thought about us. Do we think Satan won't come into our churches? Our private Christian schools? Our homeschool classes? Our church-league sports programs? Our Bible study groups? Our marriages? Our relationships? Our children's lives? Our finances? Our jobs?

Do we tend to believe that Satan stays in the dark, the evil side of life? That he stays away from organizations or people with the label "Christian"? Do we believe because we hope he doesn't come near our families, friends, homes, churches, or jobs he won't? Do we believe he resides on the other side of the tracks? And as long as we don't go looking for evil, we won't come face-to-face with him or his schemes? Do we tend to be convinced that Satan can be confined in a box only messing with those who participate in the various forms of evil or who have no belief in God? If this is our thoughts/beliefs about the enemy of our souls, then Satan is exactly where he wants us to be—deceived.

Fierce Warrioress is a six-week women's Bible study concentrated on spiritual warfare. Believers in Jesus Christ are adopted into God's family inheriting His Kingdom as well as becoming a member of His royal family; thus, given the names *Princess* and *Heiress*. Another name given to believing women in God's kingdom is *Warrioress*, which means "a female warrior," and speaks to our kingdom responsibilities (Judges 6:12).

The theme verse is Nehemiah 4:14, "Don't be afraid of the enemy! Remember the Lord, who is great and glorious, and fight for your brothers, your sons, your daughters, your wives, and your homes" (NLT). The study is divided into three parts based on the theme verse:

PART 1—Don't be afraid!
PART 2—Remember the Lord.
PART 3—And fight.

In the Old Testament, God's warriors fought battles physically—defeating enemies in hand-to-hand combat. New Testament believers are called to fight battles spiritually (Ephesians 6:12). Our enemy, Satan, is a deceiver, tempter, thief, murderer, destroyer, and accuser. Knowing his time is short, Satan "prowls around like a roaring lion, looking for someone to devour" (1 Peter 5:8, NLT). This truth is by no means meant to scare anyone. What it is meant to do is cause awareness for a battle plan.

When fighting our spiritual enemy, sometimes we are on the offensive and sometimes on the defensive. Just as one protects her home and family against intruders from an offensive position such as locking doors, turning on lights, and owning a large dog, for believers God has provided spiritual weapons of warfare to keep out the enemy. If an intruder does find his way into a home, weapons are available such as calling 911, screaming, and retrieving a gun to fight for one's life. If the enemy has wormed his way into one's life or the life of a loved one, God has spiritually given believers weapons to defeat the enemy that have "divine power to demolish strongholds" (2 Corinthians 10:4). At the end of certain days of study, you will be asked to fill in the blanks on the shield located in the back of the book which will blazon our battle plan in times of spiritual warfare. This activity serves as a practical step to help you remember what you learned especially when you have completed the study. It also serves as a tool during times of spiritual warfare that will keep you active and alert.

Fierce Warrioress examines, studies, and applies to a believer's life the tactics of war used by warriors and warrioresses who fought physical battles in the Old Testament as well as spiritual battles in the New Testament. *Fierce Warrioress* is a battle plan for women who find their lives resembling more of a battlefield rather than a theme park. *Fierce Warrioress* examines who the enemy is beginning with the Fall of Man as Adam and Eve encountered Satan in the very place they never expected—the perfect Garden of Eden. *Fierce Warrioress* addresses who God is as a mighty Warrior by studying biblical accounts. *Fierce Warrioress* provides ways to fight spiritually using biblical examples and commandments, which include praying God's Word, intercessory prayer, forgiveness, fasting, worshipping God through song, resisting, and thanking God. *Fierce Warrioress* also encourages those complacent about personal spiritual issues. Instead of complaining, doubting God, becoming depressed, or even giving up, a woman will be given the knowledge that God is with her fighting for her. We don't have to live paranoid. We can be better prepared. We will have a plan.

PART 1
DON'T BE AFRAID

*O*ur ten days of study centered on the theme of not being afraid of our enemy begins today. As you read in the Introduction, the theme verse for *Fierce Warrioress* is Nehemiah 4:14. Nehemiah was a man of God who saw the needs of God's people and volunteered to lead the families who worked at rebuilding the wall around Jerusalem since the wall was their main source of protection from the neighboring enemies. While the families worked on the wall, the enemies harassed them to the point of quitting. This is when Nehemiah stepped in and gave them the pep talk of a lifetime. The first thing he charged all the people with was, "Do not be afraid of the enemy!" Nehemiah's inspiring words are the catalyst that produced the spiritual battle plan that we too can use in the 21st century. Our study begins with getting acquainted with the enemy of all enemies, Satan. The more we learn about Satan and the more we learn about our God and the more we learn about who we are in Christ, then the fear of the enemy loses its grip. In God's Kingdom, the truth sets us free (John 8:32).

DAY 1: CRAFTY

"Now the serpent was more crafty than any of the wild animals the LORD God had made."

GENESIS 3:1a

*I*f we think we can create an environment or belong to such and such a group where we are off limits to Satan and his schemes, we have been misinformed. There was never a more perfect environment on earth than the Garden of Eden. The Garden of Eden existed after God spoke the heavens and the earth into existence. In the heavens were made the sun, moon, and stars. On the earth was made the waters, plants, trees, and animals of every kind. God, then, created male and female in the image of God, and He blessed them. Genesis 1:31 states, "God saw all that he had made, and it was very good."

It was in the Garden of Eden that God put the first man created, Adam, in charge of the land and animals. It is also the place where the first marriage union was established. Adam and the first woman created, Eve, were both so pure and innocent that being naked together brought no shame or embarrassment (Genesis 2:25). Their lives were lived with the purest bliss. They were united as one who neither knew what it meant to leave father or mother (Genesis 2:24) for the sake of the marriage vows. It was love at first sight wrapped up with the wonder of the presence of their creator God.

1. According to Genesis 2:16 God told Adam that he is free to do what?

2. What was God's command to Adam in Genesis 2:17?

At some point Adam must have shared this vital information with his new bride—that she could have all to her heart's content within the Garden of Eden—except from the one tree. From these two verses we can understand that man was created with a free will—a will to make choices for his own good or for his own harm. Man and woman were equally created in the image of God, so too are we (Genesis 1:27). God established that we bear His image by giving us a spirit (1 Thessalonians 5:23) and "the mind of Christ" (1 Corinthians 2:16). We can be similarly compared to the characterization of Jesus when He was on earth, yet He was without sin.

A mystery to us but not to the newlyweds, was talking animals. It must have been a normal thing within the Garden to talk with the animals as we will read of a conversation Eve had with a serpent. We are not sure how long the honeymoon phase lasted, but we are told in Genesis 3 that the two lovebirds had a disguised enemy watching them. Please read the fascinating encounter Eve had with a talking serpent in Genesis 3:1-7.

3. How is the serpent described?

4. Where was Eve when the serpent was talking to her?

5. Why do you think Eve was not suspicious of him?

6. How do you think the serpent knew what God had said?

The question begged to be answered is, "Who really is this serpent?" Revelation 12:9 gives us the direct answer, "The great dragon was hurled down—that ancient serpent called the devil, or Satan, who leads the whole world astray. He was hurled to the earth, and his angels with him."

7. What are the three names given to the "ancient serpent"?

This passage of Scripture in Revelation is prophetic; it has yet to come to pass. The Scripture is revealing the end of Satan and "his angels" as God showed it to the apostle John who recorded what he saw and heard in a vision (Revelation 1:1-3).

Let's take a further look at Scriptures highlighting Satan's beginnings. Throughout Scripture, especially found in the Old Testament, two meanings can be applied: one literal, and one metaphoric. This is the case in Isaiah 14:12-15 and Ezekiel 28:11-19 as it serves as a dual inference to an earthly king as well as a description of Satan before we see him on the pages of Genesis 3. Take a look at Isaiah 14:12-15.

Interesting to note that the *King James Version* uses the name *Lucifer* for "morning star."

8. How many times does the words "I will" occur in verses 13-14?

Lucifer, as Satan was originally called, was the most beautiful angel and was also the highest of all angels. He was as close to God as any created being could be. From those five statements of "I will" we can conclude that Lucifer was filled with pride; he wanted to be like God not in the sense of glorifying God, but in the worst way—to be God.

9. Since he was not God, what was the result of his pride according to verse 15?

Instead of residing in the heights of heaven, his new abode is in the depths of darkness.

Let's turn our attention to Ezekiel 28:11-19.

These Scriptures sound familiar, huh? Again, the literal meaning of this passage refers to the king of Tyre, but metaphorically it references the one "who leads the whole world astray" (Revelation 12:9).

10. This time jot down the phrase following "you were" as it occurs seven times in verses 12-15.

God ordained him in the highest position (outside the Trinity) with the utmost beauty and splendor. God's "you were" which were truly good at the time, turned into Lucifer's "I will" which is what expelled him out of the Kingdom of Light. Verse 17 states it all, "Your heart became proud on account of your beauty, and you corrupted your wisdom because of your splendor." Satan's fate is now sealed with no redemption. His choice was made. But before he enters his eternal doom to the pit of hell (Revelation 20:10), he is bent on hostility aimed at believers. He is out to deceive those who carry the name of the One whom he could never be. We have studied Scripture today giving us great insight into the origins of sin along with the origins of Satan who appeared as a talking serpent in the perfect place, the Garden of Eden.

Dear Heavenly Father, I delight in Your Word, and I desire to know and understand more. Be my Teacher.

DAY 2: DECEIVED

***

"The woman said, 'The serpent deceived me, and I ate.'"

GENESIS 3:13b

The true account of Adam and Eve and the serpent is undeniably fascinating and mysterious. Yet, it also reveals insights into our own ways of being vulnerable to Satan's deception.

I am inclined to believe that Eve had visited the tree of the knowledge of good and evil multiple times before this encounter occurred with the serpent. I can imagine Eve had a particular time in her day when she stole away from the daily routine to admire the beauty of the place God put them in and would stop and gaze at the forbidden tree. I'm sure she would walk around the tree, memorizing the colors of the particular fruit hanging from the beautiful branches. The look and smell of it must have been mesmerizing. Maybe she even talked aloud to herself wondering why God would not allow her and Adam to partake of such delight. So, here she is in a truly perfect world. She and her husband could pick from the abundance of the produce of the garden with nothing less than the ultimate harmony with creation and God. Everything was perfect . . . until she disobeyed God. If Eve sought after something that tempted her—the one thing that was forbidden—how much more are we tempted to satisfy our sinful cravings? James 1:13-15 shines a spotlight on Eve's situation as well as ours. "When tempted, no one should say, 'God is tempting me.' For God cannot be tempted by evil, nor does he tempt anyone; but each person is tempted when they are dragged away by their own evil desire and enticed. Then, after desire is concerned, it gives birth to sin; and sin when it is full-grown, gives birth to death."

1. Is there anything/anyone you desire that is without a doubt outside of God's will?

2. Do you secretly believe God is withholding something from you?

Let's go back to Genesis 3.

3. What did Satan ask Eve in Genesis 3:1?

Isn't it interesting that Satan brings up the subject of God? One would think the last person Satan would mention was God. After all, He is the One who created, provided, and cared for the newly married couple. Strange to think that speaking of God could be an advantage for Satan.

4. What could be a motive for Satan to mention God?

In Day 1, you answered the question, "Why do you think Eve was not suspicious of Satan?" In other words, how did she not know he was a "bad guy"? Eve continued to have a conversation with the serpent in verses 2-4 as if he could be trusted. He did seem to know God and what He had said to them. She had no reason not to trust him until he twisted God's words. What is important is to pause a moment and think about the situation Eve encounters so that we as women can learn from her experience. The apostle Paul warns the church at Corinth that, "Satan himself masquerades as an angel of light" (2 Corinthians 1:14). As we consider Adam and Eve's sin, which obviously affected every human being after them, let's not imagine the serpent in a red devil costume holding a pitchfork. In fact, it would be just the opposite. He must have looked nice and welcoming. The sparkle in his eye was inviting, not freaky. His voice was pleasant, not spooky. His demeanor was confident, not perverse. His interest in her was charming, not creepy. She wasn't scared off by him. Maybe the serpent, who at this point had legs (it wasn't until God cursed snakes in Genesis 3:14 that they were made to crawl), stood beside Eve and appeared to be as enticed by the tree's brilliant beauty as she was.

Answer the following questions from Genesis 3:1-6.

5. How did Eve clarify the serpent's explanation about what God had said (verse 2)?

6. What did the serpent say that God knew (verse 5)?

7. What was the outcome of the conversation in verse 6?

The serpent was definitely convincing and believable. He was out to sell Eve on the forbidden tree, and she bought it there on the spot. It was so yummy she had to share with her silent husband who apparently was just along for the ride. Adam must have known what was going on, but unfortunately refused to intrude on the conversation or Eve's disobedient actions. She saw, she took, she ate, and she gave.

Satan knew exactly what he was doing as he initiated the conversation with Eve. He had it all planned out beforehand. His plan was to outsmart Eve and lead her away from her pure and holy relationship with God. He was aware of her weakness for the tree and its fruit and subtly attacked her vulnerability by using it to twist God's word to bring about doubt and ultimately sin.

8. What emotions do you think Eve felt when she realized her eyes were now opened in a way she didn't expect (Genesis 3:7)?

Eve must have been massively confused. Partaking of the fruit and believing the serpent words ultimately did not produce the results she anticipated by any stretch of the imagination. The circumstances could not have been worse. It was all her fault. She had been tricked. She fell for the lies. She must have been angry at the serpent and herself, and yet grief stricken because the results were so far removed from what was promised. Disappointment was an understatement. The irresistible tree was now the source of such regret and shame.

9. Can you relate? Have you given in to something only later to acknowledge you were deceived? Do you remember the emotions the situation evoked?

The apostle Paul wrote about just such a thing happening to the church in Corinth: "But I am afraid that just as Eve was deceived by the serpent's cunning, your minds may somehow be led astray from your sincere and pure devotion to Christ" (2 Corinthians 11:3).

Adam and Eve walked and talked with God, Himself in the garden where He had placed them. They had an authentic, personal relationship with their Maker. There was no denying that Adam and Eve knew God and God knew them. Take time to reflect on your history with God even if you are a new believer in Christ.

10. Briefly describe the beginning of your devotion to your God and Savior.

The apostle Paul in 2 Corinthians 11:3-4 admonishes the believers to stay true to what they knew in the beginning from what was spoken to them about Jesus and to not accept any other teachings contrary to the gospel of Jesus Christ. Isn't that what the serpent spoke to Eve? He spoke words that did not match the truth of God's Word. In other words, the serpent lied. John 8:44b blatantly describes Satan, "He was a murderer from the beginning, not holding to the truth, for there is no truth in him. When he lies, he speaks his native language, for he is a liar and the father of lies." As we have educated ourselves and continue to educate ourselves on the teachings of the Bible, we need not fear we will accept lies. We have the knowledge through the Holy Spirit to "test the spirts to see whether they are from God" (1 John 4:1). The beloved disciple John spells it out plainly, "This is how you can recognize the Spirit of God: Every spirit that acknowledges that Jesus Christ has come in the flesh is from God, but every spirit that does not acknowledge Jesus is not from God . . ." (1 John 4:2-3a). My prayer is that you will recognize the voice of the deceiver and not go along with the lies.

Dear Heavenly Father, Open my spiritual eyes so I can know if I have been deceived by lies contrary to Your truth. Teach me to know truth from lies. Thank You for my pure relationship I have in You.

DAY 3: THAT ANCIENT SERPENT

"The great dragon was hurled down—that ancient serpent called the devil, or Satan, who leads the whole world astray."

REVELATION 12:9

Eve wasn't aware she had a real live enemy out to destroy her marriage, her home, her confidence, her innocence, and ultimately her relationship with her Creator. We can't allow ourselves to think the enemy doesn't come after us too. Just because you may not be thinking of Satan, doesn't mean he isn't thinking about you. Eve may not have been prepared for her day of reckoning, but ladies, we can be prepared. No need to be paranoid. In order to have a battle plan, it is critical we understand who our enemy is, who we are fighting against.

Please read Genesis 3:8-13.

1. What action did Adam and Eve take as soon as they heard the LORD God walking in the Garden?

2. Why did Adam say they were hiding?

3. According to Adam, why did he eat the fruit?

"Then the Lord God said to the woman, 'What is this you have done?' The woman said, 'The serpent deceived me, and I ate'" (Genesis 3:13). From the *Strong's Exhaustive Concordance of the Bible* the word *deceived* in Hebrew means "to lead astray, i.e. (mentally) to *delude*, or (morally) to *seduce*: beguile, deceive." Eve owned up to what she did by replying, "and I ate." She also acknowledged that she had been mentally led astray to believe a lie from the serpent. She identified her enemy but knew she, too, was accountable.

From examining Scriptures we can conclude several things at this point. First, the serpent was the agent Satan used to maneuver his way into Eve's thinking to tempt her to believe his lies instead of God's truth. Satan masqueraded as a creature (created by God) in order to deceive Eve. Second, the tree and its fruit was the bait used to lure Eve toward a new way of seeing "like God, knowing good and evil" (Genesis 3:5). Third, that Eve identified the serpent as the source of her deception. Eve came out of hiding to answer to God's authoritative question even knowing she was at fault.

Before we begin to make application, let's examine a New Testament account of a man being an agent of Satan. Read Luke 22:1-6.

4. What Jewish festivity was about to occur?

5. Who wanted to get rid of Jesus?

6. Who was Judas?

7. What did Satan do?

8. What was Judas's next step?

9. Now read Luke 22:47. What did Judas do while Jesus was speaking to the other disciples in the Garden of Gethsemane?

As we read these two entirely different accounts, it is quite obvious what Satan had done and what he was scheming through the serpent and then through Judas. But, it wasn't obvious to Eve. It also wasn't obvious to the other disciples. Luke 22:20-23 says, "In the same way, after the supper he took the cup, saying, 'This cup is the new covenant in my blood, which is poured out for you. But the hand of him who is going to betray me is with mine on the table. The Son of Man will go as it has been decreed. But woe to that man who betrays him.' They began to question among themselves which of them it might be who would do this."

Later, Judas was "seized with remorse" at what he had done to Jesus. Judas returned the payment he received for betraying Jesus to the chief priests and told them, "I have sinned." Then he hanged himself (Matthew 27:3-5).

The subject of Satan is not one that is commonly taught—not sure it is a topic that reels in the community to come to church. Maybe Satan isn't the topic of a good sermon, or the most popular character in the Bible, but he is someone we need to educate ourselves on. I am sure you have plenty of questions regarding Satan.

10. What are a few of your questions?

Do you wonder if Satan is everywhere like God? Do you wonder if he is all-knowing like God? Do you wonder if he can read your mind? Do you wonder who the demons are?

These are tough questions. If you are studying with a small group, I highly suggest these questions be discussed as you use Scriptures to back up your beliefs and not just someone else's opinion or experiences. Do some research of your own by reading commentaries and books written by credible authors.

Let's tackle the subject of demons by looking at the few Scripture references that give insight. As far as the origin of the demons, scholars reference Revelation 12:4, "Its tail swept a third of the stars out of the sky and flung them to the earth." The stars are symbolic of the angels who chose to go with Lucifer after he was expelled from heaven. A third of the angels are now the demons. Second Peter 2:4 adds, "For if God did not spare angels when they sinned, but sent them to hell, putting them into gloomy dungeons to be held for judgment." Since Satan is a created being by God, he cannot be everywhere at the same time, so he uses his agents, the demons, to aid him in his scheming. These demons are ranked just like there is a ranking of God's host of angels. Satan craftily, for use of his own evil ways, counterfeits what God does. The ranking of the demons is found in Ephesians 6:12, "For our struggles is not against flesh and blood, but against the rulers, against the authorities, against the powers of this dark world and against the spiritual forces of evil in the heavenly realms." The demons are listed as "the rulers," "the authorities," "powers of this dark world," and "the spiritual forces of evil." The "heavenly realms" refer to what our physical eyes cannot see. It refers to the realm that spirit beings roam whether it be for the kingdom of darkness or the Kingdom of Light (Job 1:7; Ephesians 2:2; Hebrews 12:1; Daniel 10:13). Yes, demons are real. And, yes, demons do Satan's dirty work of tempting us. Satan is not equal with God nor are his demons equal to God's angels. Satan's power is definitely limited as evidenced by the book of Job. Nowhere in Scripture does it state that Satan can read minds. He has been roaming since the day of Adam and Eve, so really he doesn't need to read our minds, our words and actions speak for themselves. This is one reason why it is so important we stay in God's Word and connected to a body of believers. As we study our spiritual enemy, we are gaining knowledge which will allow us to recognize and turn away from deception. We will study Ephesians 6 throughout this study, so be sure we will be coming back to the sixth chapter of Ephesians.

Dear Heavenly Father, I pray You will put a hedge of protection around me and my loved ones just as you did for Job (Job 1:10). My heart trusts in You.

Day 4: Devour

"Be alert and of sober mind. Your enemy the devil prowls around like a roaring lion looking for someone to devour."

1 Peter 5:8

1. Have you learned something new so far through the past three days of study? Have you come to understand something about God, Satan, or yourself that was unclear before?

My thoughts keep coming back to what Eve said when God asked her in Genesis 3:13, "What is this you have done?" Eve replied, "The serpent deceived me, and I ate."

It is clearer to me now that she didn't just blame the serpent for her wrong-doing, but she confessed that she ate. I believe this is an admission of owning up to her responsibility even though she was tricked into doing the wrong. She acknowledged she was "deceived," which tells me she isn't in denial of what occurred between her and the serpent. At first glance, it may appear that Eve was placing blame on the serpent, but she didn't say, "He made me," or "I didn't know what I was doing," or "It isn't my fault." She didn't even tell a little white lie to say she just had a bite. In fact, the Hebrew word translated "ate" means to "consume" or to "devour." She clearly confesses, "I ate." Eve ate the entire piece of fruit from the tree. I believe Genesis 3:13 is about the facts, not about excuses. Immediately following Eve's confession, God gives out the punishments, the curses (Genesis 3:14-19). This could also indicate Eve's guilt as God didn't have to convince Eve of her disobedience, but went straight into issuing the consequences.

2. What is Satan's job description in 1 Peter 5:8?

3. What do you learn about Satan from Ephesians 2:2?

The word *devour* is a word that literally or figuratively means "to drink down" or "to gulp entirely."[1] While Eve was devouring the fruit from the forbidden tree, Satan's plan was to devour Eve and all who would come after.

From the account of Eve and the serpent, we learn that the #1 purpose of Satan is to ruin our relationship with our Creator. Satan's plan is to capitalize on our weakness and vulnerability (based upon our earthly nature) and initiate doubt of who God is and what He has said. Then, as we begin to accept the lies from Satan, our belief system is in big-time jeopardy, meaning the decisions we make could cost us more than we could ever imagine.

4. Can you identify an area in your spiritual life where you made a poor decision because of disbelief or doubt in God or His Word?

Maybe there is a part of your life that you secretly wish God would leave you alone so that you can do as you want without any consequences. It could involve a possession, a pursuit, a habit, or even anger.

5. According to Colossians 3:5, 8, what are things that belong to our earthly nature?

6. From the list, circle the ones that have been a part of your earthly nature at any time in your life.

The #2 purpose of Satan is to ruin our relationships with those closest to us. Satan attacks relationally in marriages, parent-child, siblings, in-laws, friends, co-workers, neighbors, etc. Satan wants to isolate us from the very ones God has ordained to bring us fellowship, love, and unity.

7. Can you identify a relationship(s) in your life Satan has attacked?

8. What plan or purpose do you think Satan had in wanting discord or disunity between you and the person(s) involved?

Kay Arthur in her study, *LORD, Is It Warfare? Teach Me to Stand*, gives a genuine help in understanding our enemy, the devil, and how he uses our human vulnerabilities. She writes, "Many times beneath surface appearances an unseen, but very real, spiritual battle rages. If you've moved in Christian circles, you've heard we have three enemies: the world, the flesh, and the devil. And this is true. However, the three form a coalition, and Satan is the mastermind."[2]

We must own up to our part in our relationship with God and others where we have sinned. We are responsible for what we did or didn't do. When we confess our sin, God is faithful to forgive (1 John 1:9).

Next, we need to ask God for wisdom. God may lead us to seek counsel form someone we trust and who loves us. As we draw closer to God it will be easier to put aside our earthly nature and to take up our "divine nature" (2 Peter 1:4).

9. What qualities does the divine nature possess according to 2 Peter 1:5-7?

We've uncovered truths about who our enemy is and how he desires to destroy precious relationships. Refrain from beating yourself up over what is now obvious to you that beforehand you didn't recognize. Why does Satan use the same old tricks/schemes as he did in the Garden of Eden? Because they work! Outwit us no more, Satan! "For we are not unaware of his schemes" (2 Corinthians 2:11).

Dear Heavenly Father, open my spiritual eyes to see my real enemy. Forgive me of my sin. Give me wisdom from above.

Day 5: No Fear

"His heart is secure, he will have no fear; in the end he will look in triumph on his foes."

Psalm 112:8

As we come to the end of Week 1 of our focus on who our real enemy is, at the end of today's lesson we will be able to write our first tactic in our spiritual battle plan.

As I write this portion of this study, Halloween is approaching on the calendar. Scary creatures are appearing in neighbor's yards. Ghosts made out of white sheets inhabit one yard entirely. Oversized black cats and hairy tarantula's occupy sidewalks with a look that dares one not to come any closer. Life-size dolls imitating real-life humans erected to cause anyone near to fear being the next victim. Then, there are the "normal" evil characters such as witches, vampires, and monsters that impose fright no matter the time of year. If Satan decorated all his schemes with this type of paraphernalia–this Bible study would not even be necessary—he would be easily recognized and easily avoided. Warrioress, "be alert and of sober mind" (1 Peter 5:8a).

"The thief comes only to steal and kill and destroy; I have come that they may have life, and have it to the full" (John 10:10).

1. According to John 10:10, what specifically is the thief's (Satan) plan?

Our chiefest enemy, Satan, who deceives does not make it obvious that the end result of his plan is to rob, murder, and annihilate. His plan is the complete reversal of God's plan.

2. According to John 10:10, what is God's plan for all people?

It is a rational fear, meaning it makes logical sense, to be afraid of someone who comes *only* to bring death and destruction. That should cause a holy "Yikes!" The great news though is that is not the end of the story. A greater One has come to give us life "more abundantly" (KJV); not just "abundantly," but "more abundantly"! This same Greek word appears in Ephesians 3:20 "immeasurably more."

3. In the space below write out Ephesians 3:20.

4. Where is God's power at work?

Being a mother who always seemed to be in a hurry and made just as many messes as my children, when they were toddlers as I poured their snacks into a bowl, I would normally pour too much and have to put some back into the package. I would then comment out loud when I poured too much and say,

"Oh, that's too much." One day as I was pouring a snack into the bowl of my oldest, who was just 3 at the time, told me emphatically, "I want too much." Of course she did! Smart girl.

God gives us *too much;* he gives us more than enough. He is El-Shaddai, the All Sufficient One. John 10 reveals not just what Satan's purpose is, but it reveals God's triumphant plan and purpose as the "good shepherd" who "lays down his life for his sheep" (John 10:11). Our lives to the full and overflowing is found only in Christ who saves us (John 10:9) and provides for more than we could even begin to think about asking or imagining. In Christ we "will come in and go out, and find pasture" (John 10:9). Jesus spoke in parables often as well as identified Himself as a shepherd and believers as sheep to give us word pictures in order to help us better understand who He is in relation to us.

Let's turn our attention once more to Genesis 3. I don't want to end this week on a negative note concerning Adam and Eve as if after they sinned they were abandoned by God. Let's read Genesis 3:21-24.

4. What did God provide for Adam and Eve before he sent them out of the Garden of Eden?

5. After He sent them out of the Garden what did He provide for their protection (verse 24)?

Because our Good Shepherd provides and protects daily (Matthew 6:9-13), we need not be afraid of our enemy. "For God hath not given us the spirit of fear; but of power, and of love, and of a sound mind" (2 Timothy 1:7, KJV).

6. From the above verse, what 3 things has God generously given us?

7. What has God not given us?

From the following verses fill in the blanks with the words "will not fear."

"I _____ _____ _____ though tens of thousands assail me on every side" (Psalm 3:6).

"Though an army besiege me, my heart _____ _____ _____; though war break out against me, even then I will be confident" (Psalm 27:3).

"Therefore we _____ _____ _____, though the earth give way and the mountains fall into the heart of the sea . . ." (Psalm 46:2).

I am definitely not one to give credit to Satan where it is not due. Whatever or whomever "assails" or "besieges" us, or whatever natural disaster occurs—it is our God given right to not be afraid.

The psalmist David who was a shepherd of sheep before he became king penned God's provision and protection beautifully:

> The Lord is my shepherd, I lack nothing. He makes me lie down in green pastures, he leads me beside quiet waters, he refreshes my soul. He guides me along the right paths for his name's sake. Even though I walk through the darkest valley, *I will fear no evil* for you are with me; your rod and your staff, they comfort me. You prepare a table before me in the presence of my enemies. You anoint my head with oil; my cup overflows. Surely your goodness and love will follow me all the days of my life, and I will dwell in the house of the Lord forever.
>
> (PSALM 23, *emphasis mine*)

On the first blank of your shield in the back of your book, as our first tactic of our battle plan please write: *I will not fear.*

Dear Heavenly Father, You have given me a spirit of love, power, and of a sound mind. In Your name I will not fear.

DAY 1: WAGING WAR

"For in my inner being I delight in God's law; but I see another law at work in me, waging war against the law of my mind and making me a prisoner of the law of sin at work within me."

ROMANS 7:22-23

This is it, isn't it? This is why you picked up this book in the first place. It is because your life resembles more of a war zone or battle-field than it does a theme park. You want to glorify God completely, but sin from within and without plagues you.

1. Circle the battle(s) you struggle with on a regular basis (almost daily). Underline the battle(s) you struggle with frequently (at least once a week). Put a check mark beside the battle(s) you struggle with occasionally (twice a month).

weight	marriage	cutting	perfectionism
child/children	drugs/alcohol	homosexuality	lying
infertility	relationship	promiscuity	depression
sickness	gambling	apathy	pride
impure thoughts	pornography	materialism	idolatry
finances	shopping	obsessive	jealousy/envy
job	TV/computer	behavior	gossip
ministry	phone	anger	profanity
missions	stealing	fears	

Possibly, you are wondering if what you are experiencing is "normal." Your battle may be one you have been hiding from others or have just kept silent on the matter for fear of what others would think or say. I imagine you may be feeling very lonely and afraid. Have you believed the lie that "good Christians" don't think or act this way? Have you convinced yourself that because you have entertained wrong thoughts that this must be the real you and cannot change? Simply not true, fierce Warrioress! The non-Christian is seemingly getting away with the sin because it is still a part of his or her nature. You, Warrioress, are free from the sinful nature, which is why you are struggling. The battle goes against who you are in Christ; it is *not* who you are (1 Corinthians 5:6-7). The apostle Paul reminds us that "all have sinned and fall short of the glory of God" (Romans 3:23). But, those in Christ "are all justified freely by his grace through the redemption that came by Christ Jesus" (Romans 3:24). What separates us from the non-Christian is the grace of God we received upon salvation. His grace declares our freedom from being guilty. Paul warns believers not to take advantage of God's grace by continuing to sin (Romans 6:1-2). We saw a demonstration of the grace of God in Day 5 of Week 1 when God clothed Adam and Eve with the animal's skins He made them. He graced them. Were Adam and Eve perfect? No. Are we perfect? No. We are instructed to "not let sin reign in your mortal body so that you obey its evil desires" (Romans 6:12).

The apostle Paul brilliantly describes the struggle of not wanting to sin, but having the vulnerability to sin in his message to the Romans. Please read Romans 7:14-25.

2. What is Paul's predicament?

3. What is "living in" Paul?

4. What are Paul's desires?

5. What does Paul's mind think on? What does his flesh think on?

6. What is the solution to Paul's situation?

Warrioress, even Paul felt as if he were crazy. Be aware that what you are experiencing isn't just "normal," it is biblical. You are not crazy!

When unforeseen circumstances come upon us, sometimes our own response and/or actions can surprise even ourselves. We didn't even know we were capable of responding the way we did or acting out in the way that we did. Sometimes, something comes out of us that we didn't even know existed. Times when our flesh reacts before we even have time to pray or ask for prayer or use wisdom, are times when we can take two different paths. We can continue on the flesh-driven path, or we can take the higher road of repentance. Our flesh will tend to want to get revenge, be prideful, get defensive, speak lies, slander, gossip, give up, and so forth. The path of repentance is one of humility, love for others, taking responsibility, asking for forgiveness, correcting mistakes, and so forth.

It can be interesting how in some areas of our lives, we feel free and know we are free. But, then in another area in our lives, we feel completely defeated. Know with your mind that you are not cursed to continue in an area of bondage. In Christ, you can make the right decisions that lead to life.

Do you cry out like Paul, "What a wretched man I am! Who will rescue me from this body that is subject to death?"

7. Fill in the blank with what you desire freedom from. Who will rescue me from _____?

8. Write out Romans 7:25.

Warrioress, thank God ahead of time for His Son, Jesus Christ our Lord, who is able to set you free.

9. Has God set you free from a particular sin in the past? How are you changed?

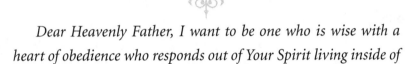

Dear Heavenly Father, I want to be one who is wise with a heart of obedience who responds out of Your Spirit living inside of me first instead of my flesh.

Day 2: Conquerors

"No, in all these things we are more than conquerors through him who loved us."

ROMANS 8:37

The *Nelson's New Illustrated Bible Dictionary* defines *war* as "armed conflict with an opposing military force. From the perspective of Hebrew people, a holy war was one that God Himself declared, led, and won. New Testament Church saw war as a spiritual battle between good and evil."[3]

God designed us, His treasured possession, to be comprised of three different and very distinct parts: body, soul, and spirit (1 Thessalonians 5:23-24). The body is our literal, physical body that requires sustenance to be maintained. The soul consists of our emotions, our personality. It is the part that reveals if one is an extravert, introvert, happy, sad, confused, etc. Our spirit is what is dead when we are physically born, but is made alive at our second birth—our spiritual birth—when we accepted Jesus Christ's invitation to follow Him. This is where the Holy Spirit then takes up residence (Titus 3:4-7).

As Christians, when the Holy Spirit indwells us, we still keep our natural, fleshly desires. Those do not magically disappear with our spiritual birth. Our goal is to surrender our will to God's will. We learn with practice and much training (just as you would for a specific sport) to have our souls come under the authority of our spirit. The times when we, like Paul, struggle with wanting to do something contrary to the will of God is when we can stop and pray and ask the Holy spirit to be in control and guide us in our decisions.

"Therefore, brothers, we have an obligation—but it is not to the flesh, to live according to it. For if you live according to the flesh, you will die; but if by the Spirit you put to death the misdeeds of the body, you will live. For those who are led by the Spirit of God are the children of God" (Romans 8:12-14).

1. In the above verse, circle the phrase "by the Spirit you put to death."
   Underline the phrase "led by the Spirit."
   Highlight the phrase "are the children of God."
   Now, write out the phrase I asked you to circle.

2. In your own words, what does that phrase mean? What do you believe God is calling you to do?

3. According to Romans 8:13, how do we as Christians accomplish what God asks of us?

A practical thing we could do to "put to death" would be to confide in an authentic friend who is also a believer that could keep you accountable to your choice to eliminate that something that needs to be gone from your daily life. Sometimes, we have to end an unhealthy relationship. Sometimes, we need someone else to go to the grocery store for us. Sometimes, we have to cut up our credit cards. Sometimes we need to stop a subscription. Sometimes we need someone to take away the phone. Please take this seriously, and know that this is a process that will take time and your commitment.

The Trinity consists of three persons, God the Father, God the Son, and God the Holy Spirit (Matthew 3:16-17; 28:19; 2 Corinthians 13:14). In the gospel of John, Jesus encourages His disciples when He educated them on His departure. In John 16:5-16, He informs them that He is about to leave them to go to His Father, but that He won't leave them empty-handed. He says that when He goes, the Spirit of Truth will come and, "will guide you into all the truth" (John 16:13). After His death, burial, and resurrection, Jesus appeared to many as a witness that truly He was the Promised One, the Messiah. He was among the people for forty days. Then, "he was taken up before their very eyes, and a cloud hid him from their sight" (Acts 1:9). The day of Pentecost soon came when the Holy Spirit filled the place where the apostles were meeting, and the Holy Spirit filled each apostle. This was in fulfillment of the prophecy, "In the last days . . . I will pour out my Spirit on all people . . ." (Acts 2:17). A crowd gathered at the amazement of the ones filled with the Holy Spirit and Peter proclaimed the good news of the gospel to the crowd. The early church was then begun. You can read further of the day of Pentecost in Acts 2.

In the Old Testament, only a selected few were privileged to be filled with the Spirit. But, this side of the cross and living with the promises of the New Testament, when one decides to follow Jesus by believing and confessing Jesus is Lord, the believer receives the gift of the Holy Spirit. The Holy Spirit takes up residence in our earthly bodies because He, "put his Spirit in our hearts as a deposit, guaranteeing what is to come" (2 Corinthians 1:22).

Some may say it would be easier to obey God and live the Christian life if Jesus was still here on earth with us. But in reality, we have the greatest privilege and honor of having Jesus' power in us through the Holy Spirit!

Romans 8:13 reveals it is "by the Spirit" we are able to "put to death." With this immeasurable, supernatural power within us, we can be more than a conqueror and put to death that which is meant to destroy us.

Sometimes we don't want to "put to death," but instead continue giving life to that part of our fleshly nature that wrongly believes "it" isn't harmful. Sometimes we want to ignore the warning signs and instead head straight to the pleasures of sin. No doubt, the flesh is alive and strong. The more you give into the destructive way, the harder it is to "put to death." This is a drastic measure in the face of drastic consequences.

Read Mark 9:43-48.

4. What is the repeated action Jesus instructs us to do if something causes us to sin?

5. In literary terms, this is known as a hyperbole; it is an exaggeration to prove a point. Jesus doesn't really ask that we cut off our feet or punch out our eyes. What do you discern Jesus' point is?

In her Bible study, *Lord Is It Warfare; Teach Me to Stand,* Kay Arthur writes, "Sin has its roots in independent action. When we choose to walk independently of God and His Word, we fall into sin. And, when we fall into sin, we are headed for the snare of the devil, unless we repent and confess our sin (2 Timothy 2:26). O Beloved, if only we understood that it is forsaken sin in the life of the believer that gives Satan a "hold"! If we could truly comprehend the truth of that reality we would quickly flee our youthful lusts!"[4]

I am convinced you value your relationship with the Lord Jesus Christ. Know that sin hinders your spiritual growth. Yes, God still loves you; nothing you do can change His love for you. In order to have worthwhile living, it is time to put to death sins that war against your spirit.

"The principle of dying to worldly systems applies beyond obvious sins. In a culture that measures everything in terms of size, success, and influence, we have to say no to these worldly values as well. In a culture of material affluence, we have to say no to coveting a better house, a sleeker car, a more upscale neighborhood, a more impressive ministry. In a culture that judges people by reputation and achievements, we have to resist the lure of living for professional recognition and advancement. Not that these things are wrong in themselves. But when they fill our hearts and define our motivations, then they become barriers to our relationship with God—which means they become sin for us. As Paul says, anything not of faith is sin, because it blocks our *single-* minded devotion to God and hinders our growth in holiness"[5]

Please read Zechariah 4:6-7. The Lord spoke through His angel to Zerubbabel who was one of the men instructed to help rebuild the temple after it had been destroyed by the Babylonians. This task of rebuilding was overwhelming, but God gently reminded him of how it would be accomplished.

6. What did God reveal to Zerubbabel?

God is in the business of tearing down and rebuilding. He uses us to do His work, which brings God the glory. Removal of entangling sin produces a life that God blesses. It also promotes a constant dialogue with our Savior, which strengthens our relationship with Him. I happen to think He loves it when we are thinking about Him and dependent upon Him. We were made to need Him. Relationship with our Creator is beautiful, natural, and romantic.

You need not fear, Warrioress, you are more than a conqueror though the power of the Holy Spirit inside you.

Dear Heavenly Father, I confess I need You. I confess I am nothing without You. Thank You for the immeasurable gift of the Holy Spirit within me.

DAY 3: LIGHT AND LAMP

"Your word is a lamp for my feet and a light on my path."

PSALM 119:105

*D*o you wish God would wave His hand over your troubles and struggles and make everything all better? Do you wish you could live on a deserted island all alone? Do you wish relationships, jobs, and just life in general could be easier? If God were to wave a magical wand over your life, you, Warrioress, would be a wimpy warrioress instead of a fierce warrioress. As a Princess, Heiress, and Warrioress, we have an ordained responsibility to God's kingdom to represent Him even when life is harder than we expected, even when we are exhausted, even when we want to give up, even when we are persecuted, and even when we don't know what to do.

"Picture the world as God's territory by right of creation. Because of the Fall, it has been invaded and occupied by Satan and his minions, who constantly wage war against God's people. At the central turning point in history, God Himself, the second person of the Trinity, enters the world in the person of Jesus Christ and deals Satan a deathblow through His resurrection. The Enemy has been fatally wounded; the outcome of the war is certain; yet the occupied territory has not been liberated. There is now a period where God's people are called to participate in the follow-up battle, pushing the Enemy back and reclaiming territory for God. This is the period in which we now live—between Christ's resurrection and the final victory over sin and Satan.

Our calling is to apply the finished work of Christ on the cross to our lives and the world around us, without expecting perfect results until Christ returns."[6]

In reading the previous quote, we needed some background orchestra music written for a dramatic movie as the heroine figures out who she is, takes her sword from her side, and races off to the fight of her life. Actually, we do have a dramatic event recorded for us in Scripture of a heroine who races off to fight for her people, God's people. Before you turn to read of the supernatural, real-life, courageous story of Deborah, why don't you cue up some climatic music as you read Judges 4 aloud? Come on, who says Bible study has to be rigid?

1. Take a look at the verbs associated with Deborah. Write the action verbs from the following verses:

    Judges 4:4 action verb

    Judges 4:6 action verb

    Judges 4:7 action verb

    Judges 4:9 action verb

    Judges 4:10 action verb

2. Another heroine emerged at the end of the story. What was her name and what unbelievably brave act did she commit?

3. What is it about these two heroines that cause you to marvel?

4. What part of the story is your favorite?

Deborah and Jael had no fear! Both stood their positions, faced the enemy, and overcame. You may be a woman or a family member of the United States Army. You may be one who has had to combat physically against a seen enemy. No doubt, there are appropriate times when using a weapon or our physical strength is needed to literally save our lives. The Bible addresses an unseen enemy who we fight not with weapons of the world but of the supernatural (2 Corinthians 10:4).

Read Ephesians 6:10-17.

5. What is our struggle not against (verse 12)?

6. What is our struggle against (verse 12)?

7. What is our sword (verse 17)?

Our struggle is not against flesh and blood, but against Satan and his demons who are of the spirit realm. We, as humans, are physical and spiritual beings. We, therefore, can use our physical bodies such as our mouths, voices, and minds to combat our unseen, spiritual enemy. You are wielding your very sword each and every time you learn Scripture, quote Scripture, memorize Scripture, pray Scripture, sing Scripture, and apply Scripture to your circumstances. We may not know what step we are to take in a particular situation. We may feel the darkness surrounding us. Just the very act of reading the Bible can illuminate God's will or allow us to be still and know that He is God (Psalm 46:10). God's Word defeats our enemy Satan and his demons every single time "because the one who is in you is greater than the one who is in the world" (1 John 4:4). This is a *spiritual* battle requiring spiritual weapons for victory. No need to fear, "His power has given us everything we need for a godly life" (2 Peter 1:3).

"The outcome of the great war is not in question. It is certain. Christ will reign victoriously forever. The only question we must answer is this: Will we fight on his side or against him? We answer this question not just once, with our words, but daily, with our choices"[7]

Dear Heavenly Father, Thank You for Your holy Word that guides and directs my very steps.

DAY 4: LOVE

"And now these three remain: faith, hope and love. But the greatest of these is love."

1 CORINTHIANS 13:13

*S*ometimes looking too far into the future is overwhelming. Thinking about 5-10 years from now is unthinkable when the present day is more than one can grasp. Just doing the right thing *today* gets you to where you desire to be 5-10 years from now.

Human nature tends to make life harder than it has to be. If you have children, I am certain you have pondered the same sentiment. Life would be so much simpler and actually fun if our children obeyed us the first time, huh? I remember when my daughters were in their toddler years. I would constantly reprimand them for the same things over and over. Some of our struggles are power struggles. It can be tough to allow someone else to make decisions concerning our lives.

1. Has obeying an authority figure (God, parents, teachers, boss, policeman, etc.) been difficult for you? Why or why not?

Our previous days of study taught us that through the power of the Holy Spirit we can be more than a conqueror, and that through the power of the Holy Spirit within us we are capable of putting to death sin. Let's take this a step further. Let's go deeper into our hearts revealing motivations.

So far we have been tackling the issues associated with our battles from a head/mind perspective using reasoning, truth, and logic. In this section, we will tackle issues directly from the heart (still utilizing truth, of course). Believe it or not, we can simply narrow the whole warzone/battlefield down to just one not so tiny topic . . . L-O-V-E.

2. Remember in Week 1, Day 5 we looked at 2 Timothy 1:7? See if you can fill in the blanks. "For God hath not given us the spirit of fear; but of _____, and of _____ and of a _____ _____" (KJV).

We already possess the ability to love. With the gift of the Holy Spirit comes the supernatural ability to love.

3. Do you already know what the first and second greatest commandments are? If not, look up Matthew 22:37-40 and record the greatest and second greatest commandments.

4. Why do you believe Jesus would pinpoint these two commands as the highest?

5. What does it look like to love God with all your heart, soul, and mind? What are practical ways to demonstrate those types of love?

6. What does the second greatest commandment look like in a practical manner of speaking?

7. In what ways can a selfless concern for others be shown?

Sometimes you just have to go back to the basics. Sometimes it is a matter of going back to square one. There are times in your life when you must go back in order to go forward.

8. Fill in the blanks for John 14:15.

    "If you _____me, _____ my commands.

It just doesn't get any simpler than that. If we really love God, we will obey.

Sometimes I feel defeated, a beat-up kind of feeling when I consider how much love is required from me. In a sense, I feel like I have already lost; so therefore, I feel as if I am excused from obedience. Other times, my love for God is so full within me that to even think about sinning is disgusting. In those times obedience is the first response instead of the "have to" response.

9. What holds you back from unabashed, unashamed, unadulterated love for God?

10. Is there something you need to let go of in order to fully love God?

11. Why is it easier to obey God when we truly love Him?

In order to be an authentic follower of the Lord Jesus Christ, in order to be a disciple, in order to obey His commands, the very first objective is to L-O-V-E Him! Instead of our prayers being filled with multiple ways to say, "Help me to obey You, Father," our prayers should be more like, "Help me to fully love You, Father." Do you see the difference? We cannot obey if we first do not love. We can determine in our heads we want to be obedient, but if our hearts, minds, and souls do not desire to love God, then we have come up against an impossible situation. It would be like getting into your vehicle with the intention of going somewhere. You are cognizant of what needs to be accomplished at your arrival and anticipate good things, but if your fuel tank is empty, you ain't goin' nowhere! You will never be able to arrive at your destination without gas in your tank.

12. What do the following verses reveal concerning God's love and our love
for Him?

John 14:21, 23

Romans 5:5

1 John 3:16-18

1 John 4:15-17

1 John 5:1-4

13. Write out 1 John 4:19.

14. What do you conclude is the meaning of loving God?

15. How does your meaning personally affect you?

Let's take this moment to adore our Heavenly Father through the first stanza of an anonymous, old, and treasured hymn, "I Love Thee."

I love Thee, my Saviour, I love Thee, my God;
I love Thee, I love Thee, and that Thou dost know;
But how much I love Thee my actions will show.

Dear Heavenly Father, may my love for You grow with each new sunrise and sunset.

Day 5: His Unfailing Love

"Let them give thanks to the LORD for his unfailing love and his wonderful deeds for humanity."

Psalm 107:8

Yesterday's subject exposed the essential ingredient to obeying God. We learned that love is the driving force behind an obedient heart. First John 4:19—"We love because He first loved us"—brings tears to my eyes. How could I not choose to love God? He has done so much, given so much, demonstrated so much, redeemed so much, beautified so much, blessed so much, and loved so much. He has done so much in my life and is my life. How could I not choose to love Him back?

1. Can you name a time in your life that God spoke directly to your heart emphasizing His love for you?

2. How has the relationship between love and obedience impacted your relationship with God?

Beth Moore tweeted: "1 thing pervades into the shadowy, shamed places of our lives with more healing than knowing God loves us. It's knowing He finds us lovable."[8]

3. According to 1 John 4:16, what do believers know and rely on?

Need proof of God's love? His great love for us is woven intricately in Scripture from Genesis to Revelation. God is love. Everything He does from giving, sending, protecting, adopting, distributing, clothing, mending, and even rebuking comes from love. It is His nature; love is who He is. He cannot make a decision concerning us absent of His love. Love is the undercurrent of His actions.

4. Read Psalm 107, noting in the space below the many ways God loves you.

5. What is the proof of God's love from the following verses?

John 3:16

Romans 5:8

Ephesians 1:4

Ephesians 2:4

Ephesians 3:18-19

1 John 3:1

1 John 4:9

If you have yet come to fully know and rely on God's love for you, please continue to search the Scriptures and to reverently ask God to reveal His love to you. Spend some time in prayer thanking God for all the wonderful deeds He has done for *you*. Our God has loved you and me with an "everlasting love." It has no beginning and no end.

6. According to 1 John 4:11, what is to be our response to God's love for us?

The *Zondervan NIV Study Bible* describes this type of love as "a selfless concern for the welfare of others." *The Bible Knowledge Commentary* explains 1 John 4:20–5:3a: "Love for the unseen God can only be concretely expressed by love for one's visible brother. Furthermore, God's command has joined together the two kinds of love—love for God and love for one's brother." In further explanation the writer states, "This love does not spring from something lovable in the person himself, but from his paternity, since everyone who loves the Father loves His child as well. Moreover, love for God's children is not mere sentiment or verbal expression, but is inseparable from loving God and obeying His commands."[9]

7. From the above commentary, from where does our love for others spring?

First John 4:12 says, "No man has at any time [yet] seen God. But if we love one another, God abides (lives and remains) in us and His love (that love which is essentially His) is brought to completion (to its full maturity, runs its full course, is perfected) in us" (AMP).

8. In reference to 1 John 4:12, if no man has yet seen God, how can we "see" God today on earth?

These fundamental truths are essential to living out our claim to know and love God. Let's break it down in simplistic form.

God loved us → We love God → We obey God → We love others → God's love is in us → Others "see" God.

Loving God means loving others. Then, through our love, God is seen.

Authenticity of being a Christian can be traced to one simple fact. Jesus told His followers, "'By this everyone will know that you are my disciples, if you love one another'" (John 13:35).

It is time to write our second tactic of our battle plan. On the second line of your shield please write: "I will choose to love."

Dear Heavenly Father, Thank You for depositing Your Holy Spirit within me. I do love You. Help me to love You with abounding love. I choose to love others and in turn reflect You.

PART 2:

REMEMBER THE LORD

The next ten days of our study concentrates on the second charge Nehemiah spoke towards the Israelites when they felt defeated and wanted to give up because of the vicious neighbors who opposed them. Nehemiah's second charge was to "remember the Lord who is great and glorious" (Nehemiah 4:14). His words are just as fitting today as they were over 2,000 years ago. Out of our own personal relationship with our Lord, we have numerous moments we can remember and recall which will encourage us in our present situations. The reading of God's Word is also a form of remembering as we apply what God has said and done to and for His people in biblical times to give precedence for our prayers. Points in the reading of God's Word will take us to the masculine side of our God who is a Mighty Warrior who wars for you and me, as well as the One in whom we find our refuge.

WEEK 3

DAY 1: LISTENING

"Whoever has ears, let him hear."

MATTHEW 11:15

*I*n secular terms, God is referred to as "the man upstairs" who "watches us from a distance" and is accused of not caring about His creation as if He sits on His throne far away and is purposely removed from humanity's needs and cares. Another catchy phrase generated by people is, "God helps those who help themselves" as if the only time God is available is when we are already active and strong. Another mistaken notion is that no one can come to God unless he or she is cleaned up first.

1. What is another example of a known, but false, worldly view of God?

Man-made ideas about God teach us lies and steer our minds away from truly knowing our personal Lord and Savior. When we get too busy in our day-to-day lives and forget to, or even neglect to, spend time in God's Word, we are more likely to believe the lies the world offers as character references to God.

The prophet Haggai reprimanded God's people, the remnant of Jews who returned to Jerusalem from exile, for their busyness at home rather than continuing the work on the temple, which was the place where they received the Word of God and worshiped. Haggai 1:9 says, "'You expected much, but see, it turned out to be little. What you brought home I blew away. Why?' declares the LORD Almighty. 'Because of my house, which remains a ruin, while each of you is busy with his own house.'"

A familiar New Testament account of busyness is found in Luke 10:38-42. Read this passage, and then, answer the following questions.

2. Whose house did Jesus stop by as He and His disciples were traveling?

3. With what was Martha distracted?

4. What kind of relationship between Jesus and Martha can be implied based on her question to Jesus concerning Mary?

5. How did Jesus describe Martha in verse 41?

6. What was Mary not doing that made Martha so irritated?

7. What did Jesus say about what Mary was doing?

Sometimes during my personal worship times as I am reading God's Word and praying, my mind begins to wander to the many things I need to accomplish for the day. It would be so easy for me to set aside my Bible and get up and be busy doing many good things. But then, I am reminded of this account of Mary and Martha. What gets to me every single time, since I am by nature a true busybody (just go no further than my husband to second that), is that it appears that Mary isn't doing anything. And, yet, at the same time she is *doing* exactly the one thing worthwhile.

8. What exactly was Mary *doing* at the Lord's feet?

That's my favorite part. She was listening. In the Greek, the word for *listening* is a verb that means "to hear (in various senses)."[10] Mary was, in fact, *doing* something. She was taking in the words of her Lord not just through her ears, but her eyes and heart. It was Mary's choice to *not* do the busy work of preparations, but instead to listen to Jesus; words which she heard with every fiber of her being. No doubt Martha could have impressed a large crowd with her endeavors. Mary, on the other hand allowed the True Giver to impress upon her words of life. "You need eyes to see and ears to hear, Jesus said to those who doubted him. It takes the mystery of faith, always, to believe, for God has no apparent interest in compelling belief"[11]

Spiritual vitality—growth and maturation—happens as we read our Bibles daily and pray. Just as we need to intake calories through food every day for the health and well-being of our bodies, our spirit needs to be fed through the Holy Spirit by studying God's Word, praying, worshipping, serving, memorizing Scripture, listening to teachings from the Word of God, meditation, and so forth for spiritual health and well-being.

9. What or who keeps you busy—too busy for God and His Word?

10. When, for whatever reason, you do not spend time in spiritual activities, how does it affect you mentally, emotionally, and spiritually?

11. Fill in the blanks to Colossians 2:6-7.

"So then, just as you received Christ Jesus as Lord, _____
to live in him, _____ and _____ _____ in him,
strengthened in the faith as you were _____, overflowing with
_____."

12. What is the main message to Christians in Hebrews 6:1 and 1 Peter 2:2?

Oh, to be still enough; to refrain from busyness; to drown out the daily noises of the dishwasher, washing machine, phone, TV, radio, computer, and voice-mail. Oh, to take off the headphones on our head and the ear buds out of our ears. In order to hear the voice of the Lord tenderly speak words of life into our spirits to give wisdom, insight, peace, and hope, we must have ears that can actually hear!

Every time I am a facilitator for a Bible study at my church, during the first meeting where the participants introduce themselves, I ask: Why are you here? The number one response is that if they were not in a study they would not be in God's Word.

As you and I stand on the battlefield engaged in a spiritual war fighting our enemy of our spiritual health, mental health, physical health, relationships, finances, career, callings, or in whatever capacity you may be facing, one of the most important things we must do is STAY IN GOD'S WORD. It is our sword for heaven's sake! A warrioress does not leave home without her sword. Let's get the Word of God into our hearts and minds and be ready at any moment to use it.

Rick Warren in his best-selling book, *The Purpose Driven Life,* describes God's Word: "The Bible is far more than a doctrinal guidebook. God's Word generates life, creates faith, produces change, frightens the Devil, causes miracles, heals hurts, builds character, transforms circumstances, imparts joy, overcomes adversity, defeats temptation, infuses hope, releases power, cleanses our minds, brings things into being, and guarantees our future forever! We cannot live without the Word of God! *Never* take it for granted. You should consider it as essential to your life as food. Job said, 'I have treasured the words of his mouth more than my daily bread.'"[12]

One of my favorite verses to pray before reading my Bible is Psalm 119:18— "Open my eyes that I may see wonderful things in your law." The psalmist continues to declare, "How sweet are your words to my taste, sweeter than honey to my mouth" (v. 103).

Fill in the blank with your name.

 has chosen what is better, and it will not be taken away from her (taken from Luke 10:42).

Dear Heavenly Father, forgive me for the times I have neglected Your Word. I truly understand it is just as important—even more important—as the food I eat. Open my spiritual eyes and ears so that I may see and hear all the good things You have for me.

Day 2: Remember

"Remember the former things, those of long ago; I am God, and there is no other; I am God, and there is none like me."

Isaiah 46:9

Having an intimate, close, personal, and daily relationship with the Lord is a choice we must deliberately make as we go about our busy schedules. Spending time listening and reading God's Word is also important so that we have something to remember about our Lord—who He is and what He has done in the past personally and biblically. Philip Yancey wrote in *Rumors of Another World,* "Astonishingly, the Creator seldom imposes himself on his creatures. It requires attention and effort on our part to 'remember your Creator,' because the Creator slips quietly backstage. God does not force his presence on us. When lesser gods attract, God withdraws, honoring our fatal freedom to ignore him."[13]

Something so basic, so elementary, so simple, and yet can be so neglected in a Christian's life is the incredible privilege of spending time with our Creator one-on-one. Living this side of the cross means we have access to the throne of God 24/7/365 for Jesus Himself is our Mediator, our High Priest (Hebrews 8:1-2). I am convinced that the unseen world of darkness knows how valuable our alone worship times are and distracts us away from the intimate moments with our Creator. Our Lord also knows and understands how easy it is for us as humans to be distracted by what is seen and how easily forgetful we are.

1. Why do we so often forget and neglect this privilege?

Jesus' disciples were also known to be forgetful. In the gospel of Mark, the disciples not only witnessed the feeding of the 5,000, but also actually were the ones who picked up the 12 baskets of leftovers when the meal began with just five loaves of bread and two fish (Mark 6:33-44). So, after they leave the scene of the miracle, the disciples get on a boat where a terrible storm caused them to fear for their lives. Jesus comes to them by walking on the water (another miracle) and gets in the boat when the storm ceases. The disciples are said to be "sore amazed" (KJV) "for they had not gained any insight from the *incident* of the loaves, but their heart was hardened" (Mark 6:52, NASB). This amazement they experienced was not the high-five, congratulatory type of excitement, but rather, it was the feeling of disbelief. Lord, have mercy on us! May our generation be ones to actually consider Your miracles and believe.

2. What were God's chosen ones to remember? Write the word *remember* in the blanks of the following verses.

"_____ the day you stood before the LORD your God at Horeb, when he said to me, 'Assemble the people before me to hear my words so that they may learn to revere me as long as they live in the land and may teach them to their children'" (Deuteronomy 4:10).

"_____ that you were slaves in Egypt and that the LORD your God brought you out of there with a mighty hand and an out stretched arm" (Deuteronomy 5:15).

"But do not be afraid of them; _____ well what the LORD God did to Pharaoh and to all Egypt" (Deuteronomy 7:18).

"_____ the wonders he has done, his miracles, and the judgments he pronounced" (1 Chronicles 16:12).

"My soul is downcast within me; therefore I will _____ you from the land of the Jordan" (Psalm 42:6).

"On my bed I _____ you; I think of you through the watches of the night" (Psalm 63:6).

"I will _____ the deeds of the LORD; yes, I will _____ your miracles of long ago" (Psalm 77:11).

"_____ those earlier days after you had received the light, when you endured in a great conflict full of suffering" (Hebrews 10:32).

I can think of several benefits for the act of remembering. (1) It takes my eyes off me and onto my Lord, (2) It keeps me from feeling alone, (3) It causes me to be grateful, (4) It increases my faith, and (5) It motivates me to stay in relationship with my Lord.

3. What would you add to the above list?

4. Do you have a history with God? Does your family have a history with God? Take this moment right now to remember what God has done for you and/or your family. Part of what it means to remember is actually to record or write it down. Use the space below to write out some memories.

If we only knew just how powerful those written memories are to the seen and the unseen world. What you just wrote down is like dynamite that destroys lies, doubts, confusion, heresy, and unbelief. It is the light that dispels the darkness. God is definitely on your side fighting for you; you are not alone.

5. Revelation 12:11 reveals how powerful our testimony is. What two things overcome Satan?

If you were not able to record much history with God, then start your history today by journaling God's wondrous acts—big or little—from this day forward. Because of my alone worship times with God, I am then more able to recognize the presence of God in my daily activities; He becomes present and real and near. Even going to church and singing worship songs and hearing the message from my pastor has more meaning and depth when I chose that week to spend time in God's Word even if it was only for 10-15 minutes a day.

Moses was a man of God who devoted much of his time to preserving the miracles and wonders God performed for the Israelites as he meticulously wrote the first five books of the Bible, known as the Pentateuch. Praise God men like Moses obeyed the voice of God and recorded the biblical events for all generations to come.

"Only be careful, and watch yourselves closely so that you do not forget the things your eyes have seen or let them fade from your heart as long as you live. Teach them to your children and to their children after them" (Deuteronomy 4:9).

6. Underline the part in Deuteronomy 4:9 that Moses instructs what we should not forget or fade from our heart.

7. What does Moses say our responsibility is to the things we have seen with our eyes?

My maternal Grandpa, Dr. Charles E. Green, was well-known in Lawton, Oklahoma for being the first pediatrician in southwest Oklahoma and for being Lawton High's football team physician for more than 40 years. He was also an ordained minister who performed so many marriages and funerals—too many to count! He was able to not only record and tell his children and grandchildren what God had done for him, but he was also granted the awesome privilege of having his life-story published in his autobiography, *The Lord Heard My Cry*.[14] My Grandpa's memory was impeccable. Until the day he died, he could recall names and dates and details as if the events had just occurred. He could remember because he never forgot; he never let the things he had seen with his very own eyes "fade from his heart." Every time we visited him and Grandma, we were retold story after story of what God had done for him and was still doing in his life. My Grandma used to try and stop him from telling so many stories thinking we didn't want to hear. But, actually, we loved hearing those stories; he was being obedient to the call of the Lord to tell them to his children and grandchildren.

Dear Heavenly Father, bless my memory. Remind me through Your Holy Spirit (John 14:26) of Your many ways You have spoken to me and revealed Yourself to me. May I be faithful to record and recount Your mercies and faithfulness to future generations.

DAY 3: KNOW

"I know that the LORD is great, that our Lord is greater than all gods."

PSALM 135:5

Have you ever had the opportunity to study the names of God? Did you know there are more than 100 names for our one God throughout the Old and New Testament? God specifically chose to reveal His character through His names in the timeliest manner to show Himself to His people. For instance, God was revealed as *Jehovah-jireh,* "The Lord Will Provide," when Abraham obediently went to offer his only son, Isaac, as a sacrifice to God on Mount Moriah. Just as soon as Abraham lifted his knife, God spoke to Abraham and provided him with a ram as a substitute sacrifice (Genesis 22). Another example is when Hagar, Abraham and Sarah's maidservant, found God to be "The One Who Sees," *El Roi,* when God found her after she ran away from Sarah who had mistreated her. Hagar responded to God's comfort and news of her being with child by proclaiming, "I have now seen the One who sees me" (Genesis 16:13).

1. Can you recall a biblical story in which a name of God is revealed? Write an example.

If you want to get to know God, get to know His name. For those fearing the enemy, fearing God should be first. As we spend time learning about who our God is and remembering what we have learned, the fear we feel toward our enemy will be lessened.

Nehemiah in Nehemiah 4:14 referred to God as "Lord." This Hebrew word for *Lord* is *Adonai*, which means "Master." Nehemiah was reminding the Jews of whom their true, one and only Boss is. He could have used the name for God that represented the covenant relationship with God by referring to God as LORD (translated *YHWH* and means "He alone is God"), but instead used *Adonai*.

2. Why do you think it is important to distinguish the two names of God—Lord and LORD—especially as it applies in Nehemiah 4:14?

Paradoxically, we serve a God who has numerous names, and yet is one.

3. Write out Deuteronomy 6:4:

4. The postexilic prophet, Zechariah, prophesied about the coming of the Day of the Lord. What did he say will be on that day in Zechariah 14:9?

In the gospel of John, Jesus prayed aloud to His Father, "that they may be one as we are one" (John 17:11). Let there be no confusion; there is ONE GOD. Humanity has made gods as objects of worship and is making gods and will continue making gods, but none will last.

5. Fill in the blanks for Matthew 6:24.

   "No one can _____ two _____. Either you will hate the _____ and love the other, or you will be _____ to the one and _____ the other."

6. Why do you think Jesus issued this warning? How does the warning apply to modern times?

The issue of whom or what is ruling over us is one that needs to be decided today, if it has not already. We must know who we serve and not be wishy-washy or double-minded.

7. According to James 1:8, what is the outcome of a double-minded (one who cannot make up his or her mind and agree on one thing) person?

Jesus asked His disciples and followers as He taught, "Why do you call me, 'Lord, Lord,' and do not do what I say?" (Luke 6:46).

8. Is God your Lord, your Master? Is He your ultimate Boss? Do you obey Him even when it is uncomfortable and is the complete opposite of what you *feel* like doing?

Kay Arthur, in *Lord, I Want to Know You* explains what it means to have God as your Lord, "The lordship of God means His total possession of me and my total submission to Him as Lord and Master."[15]

9. If you haven't yet determined that God is your Lord, your Master, what hinders your "total submission"?

Students wait their entire schooling years to turn the magical age "18" so that they can finally make their own decisions and do what they want to do without parental supervision. They daydream and anticipate their lives with so much freedom like a bird leaving the mother's nest. What they can't begin to envision is the pile of bills, the exhausting work schedules, the lack of gasoline in the car, and the endless expectations of friends and family.

10. Do you remember a time when you daydreamed about being your own boss? What did you long for?

Since I have already confessed to be a busybody, I will also confess that if I don't get the things done on my "to do" list for the day, then I become an irritable mom who sees no one else's needs but my own.

Surrendering even our wants to our Lord is a huge part of our submission. When we awake each morning, may our mouths and heart speak like Mary, the mother of Jesus, "I am the Lord's servant. May your word to me be fulfilled" (Luke 1:38).

Let this be our statement of declaration and our prayer for today and always, "But as for me and my household, we will serve the LORD" (Joshua 24:15).

Day 4: Great and Awesome

"He is the one you praise; he is your God, who performed for you those great and awesome wonders you saw with your own eyes."

DEUTERONOMY 10:21

Are you having one of those days you don't want to get out of bed? One of those days you want to bury your head in the sand and not come up until you know the coast is clear? One of those days that has defeat written all over it? A day you know you haven't the strength the work requires of you. Lies fill your mind, repeating that you are not any closer to your battle being over and none of it matters anymore anyway.

If you have one of these kinds of days, do not give up! Days like these will come. Days like these are just what our enemy is hoping for. Instead of taking a dose of his prescription, let's order him, with the authority Jesus has given us, out of our business. Wave your white flag toward your Deliverer. The white flag is an international sign of surrender; it means a ceasing of resistance. Today will be one of those days by the choice of your will, putting feeling aside, to listen to your Commander in Charge, stay close to Him, and watch Him perform wonders . . . wonders just for you.

Nehemiah's charge to his fellow men is just what we need not forget, "Remember the Lord, who is great and awesome" (Nehemiah 4:14).

If you are familiar with the Old Testament, you know that Nehemiah's charge to fight for what was already theirs was not the first time the Israelites had been in that position. After the Israelites were delivered from the hand of the Egyptians and after their 40 years of wandering in the desert, Moses commissioned God's people to fight for the land and make it their home—the Promised Land.

1. Through the prophet Moses, God spoke His heart and answered the question of why He delivered the Israelites out of slavery in Egypt. According to Deuteronomy 7:6-8, why did God deliver them?

2. What is promised in this "good land" for God's people in Deuteronomy 8:7-9?

3. How are the nations described in Deuteronomy 7:17?

Your circumstances may seem insurmountable. The Israelites could relate as they too felt as if they were in a losing position.

4. In response to this question, what does Moses remind them in verse 18?

5. Write Moses' words in Deuteronomy 7:21.

The nations/enemies that were larger and stronger than the Israelites were the exact ones God would drive out with the cooperation of His people. As the Israelites went into battle to possess the very land God ordained them to have, they had to literally fight against the ones who occupied that territory. Verses 22-23 states, "The LORD your God will drive out those nations before you, little by little. You will not be allowed to eliminate them all at once, or the wild animals will multiply around you. But the LORD your God will deliver them over to you, throwing them into great confusion until they are destroyed."

6. The Israelites's job was to annihilate their enemies as well as what according to verse 5?

7. What do you learn about God from these verses in Deuteronomy 7?

This concept of "driving out" is a reoccurring theme throughout the Old Testament (Exodus 6:1; 23:30; 34:24; Leviticus 18:24; Numbers 33:55; Joshua 17:18; Jeremiah 49:2; Ezekiel 11:7; Hosea 9:15).

The concept of "driving out" is also a reoccurring them throughout the gospels of Jesus Christ (Matthew 7:22; 8:31; 10:8; 12:28; 17:19; Mark 3:15; 7:26; 9:18; 9:28; 16:17; Luke 19:45).

Remember the believers in the Old Testament fought literal, physical battles, where the New Testament believers fight in the spiritual realm. Remember, also, our ultimate enemy is the devil and the fallen angels who serve him and are identified as demons.

8. What authority did Jesus give His disciples in Matthew 10:1 and Mark 3:15?

9. As good news of the kingdom of God was preached, what actions accompanied the messages in the following verses?

Matthew 10:7-8

Mark 3:14-15

Luke 8:1-2

He has you on His mind today. You, too, are the one God loves and considers His "treasured possession." What concerns you, concerns your heavenly Father. Isaiah 49:15-16 says, "Can a mother forget the baby at her breast and have no compassion on the child she has borne? Though she may forget, I will not forget you! See, I have engraved you on the palms of my hands; your walls are ever before me."

9. What is proof from the verse in Isaiah that God will never forget you?

As a member of God's royal family, what is God's is also ours. Our inheritance is not just something that is waiting for our arrival in heaven; our inheritance began the moment the Holy Spirit took up residency in our bodies, which is now called the temple of God (2 Corinthians 6:16). The apostle Paul reminded the believers in Ephesus of their inheritance and of their "incomparably great power" (Ephesians 1:19), as well as their position.

10. According to Ephesians 2:6 where has God seated us with Christ?

"So, although we still walk on Earth, we need to remember that we're seated in the heavenlies, and we need to live accordingly. 'Seated in the heavenlies' is not a dimensional position but a position of authority and power. If we hold our position, victory is assured despite the fierceness of the battle or the power of the enemy."[16]

Kay Arthur reminds us of our dual citizenship - one on earth and the other in heaven (Philippians 3:20). She also brings to our attention the authority we have since the Holy Spirit indwells us. Jesus told His disciples that anyone who has faith in Him will "do even greater things" than what Jesus did when He was on earth (John 14:12). Sometimes, we just need to take God up on what He says we can do.

God wrote our names on the palm of His hand; it is impossible for Him to forget us. Maybe it is our turn to do something to help us never to forget who He is and what He has done for us.

Dear Heavenly Father, I wave my white flag of surrender towards You, knowing I cannot lose being on Your side. Thank You for giving me power through the Holy Spirit against evil.

DAY 5: THE STONE

"The stone the builders rejected has become the cornerstone; the LORD has done this, and it is marvelous in our eyes."

PSALM 118:22-23

*T*he supernatural is, and pretty much has been since time began, an intriguing and fascinating subject about which persons of all ages have curiosities. Things pertaining to the supernatural are the theme of many TV shows as well as movies. The supernatural is the underlying theme of the common and popular "good versus evil" archetype. It is the battle between the good guy and the bad guy. The supernatural is of the heavenlies; it is the kingdom of light against the kingdom of darkness.

1. When you hear the word *supernatural* what comes to your mind?

Dictionary.com defines *supernatural* as:

1. of, pertaining to, or being above or beyond what is natural; unexplainable by natural law or phenomena; abnormal.
2. of, pertaining to, characteristic of, or attribute to God or a deity.
3. of a superlative degree; preternatural: *a missile of supernatural speed.*

4. of, pertaining to, or attributed to ghosts, goblins, or other unearthly beings; eerie; occult.[17]

One of the earliest books published soon after the invention of the printing press was the book *Daemonologie* by King James I (who commissioned the Bible known as the *King James Bible*). It is said that King James heard rumors that witches wanted to kill him, so in response, he researched the topic of the supernatural in the evil realm and the published book was the result.

During this time in the mid-to-late 15th century, William Shakespeare wrote the tragedy play, *Macbeth,* in hopes of entertaining the king. In the play, Shakespeare incorporated the supernatural by involving witches, including Hecate the goddess of witchcraft. At the end of the play, the "bad guys" call upon the forces of wickedness to commit murder, while the "good guys" call upon God to fight and conquer the bad guys. And, yes, the good guys, represented by the country of England, won.

Unarguably the greatest supernatural activity known to man has to be when our Lord Jesus rose from the dead. Is this not single-handedly the main difference between the One and Only God and all the other gods men worshipped and still worship today? Our God is alive. If you believe in the inerrancy of the Bible, you know that the story of the resurrected Savior is far from a folklore, fairytale, or fictional story. It is the greatest story ever told that which defines our core beliefs and on what our future rests. The Old Testament believers put their faith in the belief of the coming Messiah who would take away the sins of the world (Genesis 15:6, John 1:29); they looked forward to the day. New Testament believers, including us, put our faith in the belief that the Messiah did come who is Jesus Christ, and that He "died for our sins according to the Scriptures, that he was buried, that he was raised on the third day according to the Scriptures" (1 Corinthians 15:3-4).

All four gospels retell the supernatural event of Jesus' death, burial, and resurrection (Matthew 27:4–28:10; Mark 15:33–16:8; Luke 23:44–24:11; John 19:28–20:18). Let's turn our attention to the account written by Matthew, one of Jesus' disciples, who made it his point throughout his gospel to prove to his Greek Jewish readers that Jesus was truly who He said He was—the Son of God. Turn now and read Matthew 27:50–28:10.

2. Which holiday do we normally hear the reading of the resurrection of Jesus?

3. Was there a part of Matthew's account that you had forgotten or was new to you? If so, which part?

The four gospels each add a different detail of the resurrection story. I had not remembered here in Matthew's account of when the earthquake shook the earth exactly when Jesus died on the cross, and then, "bodies of many holy people who had died were raised to life" (Matthew 27:52). His death brought life even before He was raised from the dead on the third day.

4. What was rolled in front of the entrance to His tomb (verse 60)?

5. Why was the tomb to be made extra secure (verses 63-64)?

6. How was it made more secure (verses 65-66)?

7. Who were the first to go to Jesus' tomb the morning of the third day (verse 28:1)?

Mark's gospel adds a detail about the women who went to Jesus' tomb that morning. He recorded a part of their conversation: ". . . they were on their way to the tomb and they asked each other, 'Who will roll the stone away from the entrance to the tomb?" (Mark 16:2b-3). The women came to the tomb because they were going to anoint Jesus' body with the spices and perfumes they had prepared (Mark 16:1, Luke 23:56). These women who were devoted to Jesus were there when Jesus died on the cross (Mark 15:40-41) and saw where He had been buried (Mark 15:47). That morning they were not looking for a miracle. They thought they would encounter the dead body of Jesus. They had a huge hurdle, a not so obscure obstacle to get passed—the stone—before they could do what was in their hearts to do for the One they loved. The stone was man's idea to keep Jesus dead as if the God of the universe was limited to natural means. Little did anyone know that the stone would become a miracle.

8. Is there a "stone" between you and Jesus? Is there something in your life that is bigger than your strength that you need removed? Or, what is a seemingly impossible situation that keeps you from fulfilling what God has put in your heart to do?

Another man of God was supposedly put to his death with a stone rolled to keep him under the grip of death. A decree had been issued to the residents of Babylon by King Darius that anyone caught praying to any other god besides the king would be thrown into a den of lions (Daniel 6:7). Daniel, a Jew, was soon caught praying to God, and despite the king's personal preference, Daniel was thrown into the lion's den to what would naturally be his death (Daniel 6:16). Then, "a stone was brought and placed over the mouth of the den, and the king sealed it with his own signet ring and with the rings of the nobles, so that Daniel's situation might not be changed" (Daniel 6:17). Please read the dramatic ending after Daniel was sealed in the lion's den in Daniel 6:18-28.

9. How did God rescue Daniel?

Was the stone able to keep Jesus in the grave? No! Was the stone able to keep Daniel's situation from changing? No! The God we know, love, and serve is alive and able to rescue you from whatever seems to keep you from living life to the fullest. In Christ your life will resemble life, not death. Remember from yesterday's study that the Israelites confessed that their enemies appeared larger and stronger than themselves, but God delivered them. Whatever "stone" was meant to keep you spiritually dead will be the very stone that God rolls away to bring you back from the dead to life eternal. The stone will become your miracle story. "For God so loved the world that he gave his one and only Son, that whoever believes in him shall not perish but have eternal life" (John 3:16). It is our Enemy who wants to us to believe God won't do anything for you; that it is a situation that cannot be changed. Warrioress, remember what God supernaturally did for Daniel and for His own Son, Jesus Christ. Don't listen to the voices that speak death and hopelessness. Listen to the voice of the Holy Spirit who speaks words of life. Jesus said, "I am the resurrection and the life. The one who believes in me will live, even though they die; and whoever lives by believing in me will never die. Do you believe this?" (John 11:25-26).

For the third blank on our shield for our battle plan write the words: "I will listen to my Lord."

Dear Heavenly Father, Give me courage and strength as I believe You are my Rescuer and the One who can roll the stone away.

DAY 1: HE WILL NOT

"Do you not know? Have you not heard? The LORD is the everlasting God, the Creator of the ends of the earth. He will not grow tired or weary, and his understanding no one can fathom."

ISAIAH 40:28

This week our focus will cover the Lord as a warrior who was and is and will continue to be active in the lives of His children who depend upon Him, who hope in Him, who trust in Him, who seek His help, and whose lives rest in His deliverance.

He is here for you, Warrioress; you are not alone in this battle. You have come this far—don't give up now. Good news is ahead!

Remember the fierce warrioress, Deborah, from Week 2, Day 3? She was chosen as a judge for the Israelites, who with the help of Barak, defeated the enemy Sisera. On the day of victory, Deborah and Barak sang a song of praise because the battle was won through the hand of the Lord in Judges chapter 5.

1. What do the singers at the watering places sing about (Judges 5:11)?

2. Why is it important to remember the "victories of the Lord"?

Remembering and reciting what God has done for you and for His people is a very powerful activity that produces hope in any person's soul no matter how defeated one may feel. The hymns of the past and the worship songs of today are rich with God's victories and attributes that when sung infuses a newness or a refreshment that dissolves worry, fear, and doubt like sugar to sour lemonade. After remembering and reciting the goodness of the Lord, one cannot help but be a ray of sunshine to those "who walk along the road" (Judges 5:10) and infuse a bit of hope into their weary bodies. Hope is contagious!

3. Can you recall a time when you didn't feel like singing, but once you did begin to sing, your countenance and attitude changed for the better?

Even our posture can straighten up, huh? Our shoulders no longer droop, our chins are no longer glued to the bottom of our necks, our eyes are no longer staring down at our shoes, and our stomachs no longer stick out over our buttoned pants. We are prettier as we straighten up our spines; shoulders are back, chins high, eyes toward the heavens, and stomachs in. We could even burn a few calories as we start to sway to the music and lift our hands in praise to the One worthy of our praise and adoration.

Before we leave Deborah and Barak's song, you have to read the part when Jael killed the enemy with just one swing of a hammer in Judges 5:24-27.

4. If you could take a tent peg and a hammer to something (not a someone), what would you want to destroy instantly?

Deborah and Barak were not the first to pen their own lyrics of praise to God for deliverance from their enemies. Another male/female duo wrote an original song after God delivered the Israelites from the hands of the Egyptians. Moses and his sister, Miriam, told their story through song in Exodus 15:1-18.

5. How is God described in verses 3, 7, and 11?

6. Notice in verse 2 how personal Moses and Miriam claim God to be. Write the five attributes preceded by the pronoun "my."

7. The enemy of God's people was stubbornly arrogant. What was the enemy thinking according to verse 9?

It is just like our enemy—Satan knows he doesn't stand a chance but still attempts to get us to think he is going to overtake us.

Verse 3 reads, "The LORD is a warrior; the LORD is his name." He isn't a sissy. He is the Conqueror. He is the Bravest of the brave. He is the Champion of champions. He truly is the Ultimate Fighter. No one compares to our Warrior LORD.

The Song of Moses was not just sung in the synagogues, but is also a song that echoes in heaven. Revelation 15:2-3 reveals what John heard and saw, "I saw something like a sea made of glass, the glass all shot through with fire. Carrying harps of God, triumphant over the Beast, its image, and the number of its name, the saved ones stood on the sea of the glass. They sang the Song of Moses, servant of God; they sang the Song of the Lamb."

8. Take a look at today's verse. What can we know about God from Isaiah 40:28?

9. What do these attributes about our God mean to you?

Our God "will not grow tired or weary." He will not!

10. In the following verses write the words "He will not" in the blanks provided.

"When the LORD goes through the land to strike down the Egyptians, he will see the blood on the top sides of the doorframe and will pass over that doorway, and ___ ___ ___ permit the destroyer to enter your houses and strike you down" (Exodus 12:22-24).

"For the LORD your God is a merciful God; ___ ___ ___ abandon or destroy you or forget the covenant with your ancestors, which he confirmed to them by oath" (Deuteronomy 4:31).

"He will respond to the prayer of the destitute; ___ ___ ___ despise their plea" (Psalm 102:17).

"___ ___ ___ let your foot slip—___ who watches over you ___ ___ slumber" (Psalm 121:3).

"No temptation has overtaken you except what is common to mankind. And God is faithful; ___ ___ ___ let you be tempted beyond what you can bear. But when you are tempted, he will also provide a way out so that you can endure it" (1 Corinthians 10:13).

"God is not unjust; ___ ___ ___ forget your work and the love you have shown him as you have helped his people and continue to help them" (Hebrew 6:10).

8. Which one of these "He will not" statements mean the most to you right now in this particular season of your life? Why?

Make God your personal God too. For our prayer today, write out a prayer to God declaring your "my's" of who God is to you like Moses and Miriam did. Maybe you could put a tune to it and turn it into a song!

DAY 2: AN ARM

"Do you have an arm like God's, and can your voice thunder like his?"

JOB 40:9

G od asks Job two questions in Job 40:9. The obvious answer to both of those questions is a resounding "no!"

Our Man of War, the Warrior, is the ultimate "Man's man." His strength is so mighty that "He moves mountains without their knowing it" (Job 9:5). His power is so awesome that "He shakes the earth from its place and makes its pillars tremble" (Job 9:6). He is so fierce that "He performs wonders that cannot be fathomed, miracles that cannot be counted" (Job 9:10). Job testifies about His God, "If it is a matter of strength, he is mighty"(Job 9:19). His right arm alone could out power any and all forces that oppose Him or one of His children: "The LORD's right hand has done mighty things! The LORD's right hand is lifted high; the LORD's right hand has done mighty things" (Psalm 118:15b-16).

Remember Moses and Miriam's song? They confessed it was the Lord's power that really defeated the best of the best.

1. Read Exodus 15:3-8. What body part of the Warrior is mentioned in verse 6 and how was it used?

2. Now look at verse 12. What happened when the Warrior stretched out His arm?

3. According to Exodus 6:6, how would God redeem the Israelites?

4. Before Moses and the Israelites were even delivered entirely from slavery, Moses witnessed God doing what with His hand in Exodus 3:20?

The psalms are prayers and songs very similar to the songs of our male/female duets—Moses and Miriam, Deborah and Barak. The psalms tell a personal account of God's glorious and mighty sovereignty from the view of those who experienced relationship with God.

5. According to the following verses, what did God's right hand do?

   Psalm 17:7

   Psalm 20:6

   Psalm 98:1

Psalm 89:10, 13

Psalm 138:7

I believe this insight of God's right hand gives us permission to pray differently. When praying for a particular situation or person or for yourself, ask God to stretch out His right arm executing His supernatural power in the situation. We may not see instantaneous results, but it doesn't hurt to ask. Know that He is working even when we cannot see it yet. Praying for God to use His right arm is a part of remembering what God has done for those in the past and asking Him to do the same on your behalf. Never forget, Warrioress, He is fighting for you and with you.

God isn't "out there" somewhere fighting in a distant, unknown, heavenly territory. When He is actively fighting as a Warrior on your behalf, know He is literally by your side. You are fighting with Him. Remember one of His "will not" promises is that He will never leave us nor forsake us (1 Chronicles 28:20).

Read Deuteronomy 20:1-4. The book of Deuteronomy was written by the godly man, Moses, and showcases the very personal, close, and authentic relationship between Moses and his God.

6. Moses heard God and led His people from the exact words he heard from God. According to Deuteronomy 20:1-4, what is the emotion of the Israelites as they prepare for war?

7. What reason does God give that subdues their fear?

The Warrior goes with you, fights for you, and gives you victory. He goes "with" and fights "with" you. I want you to notice that God does His part and we do our part. He doesn't sit back and watch us fight alone, just as we don't sit back and watch Him fight alone. We are both active in the spiritual war. He leads, we follow.

Going back to the song of Moses and Miriam, I want you to look closely at the activity of God and the activity of His people. Keep in mind the purpose the song was written and sung. The Israelites were released from slavery, but they still had to literally walk away from Egypt toward the Promised Land. So, as God led them, the Red Sea was in front of them and the best of Pharaoh's army was behind them. It looked like a hopeless situation. It appeared God had brought them out of slavery only to die. They had no clue He was about to perform one of the most memorable and infamous miracles. The song commemorates the hours it took to get the thousands across the bottom of the dry sea to the other side.

8. Read Exodus 15:10-18. Now, turn your attention to verse 13. What will God do for them?

Yes, Moses sings that God "will lead" and "will guide" them. He is right there with His people going before them and leading the way as is the mark of a true Warrior and King.

Okay, stay with me. We have seen that He fights for us with His right hand, and yet He is also with us leading us. One, pretty remarkable, job of ours is something we bravely choose to do in the midst of battles.

9. In the blanks of the following verses write: "my right hand."

"I keep my eyes always on the LORD. With him at ____ ____ ____, I will not be shaken" (Psalm 16:8).

"Yet I am always with you; you hold me by ____ ____ ____" (Psalm 73:23).

10. In the blanks for the following verses write: "your right hand".

"The LORD watches over you—the LORD is your shade at ____ ____ ____" (Psalm 121:5).

"For I am the LORD your God who takes hold of ____ ____ ____ and says to you, Do not fear; I will help you" (Isaiah 41:13).

It doesn't get any sweeter than that! If we could only see with our physical eyes this side of heaven. For now, by faith we believe and see with our spiritual eyes that He leads and guides us. He goes before us fighting with His right hand, all the while, holding with His other hand our right hand where we take refuge beside Him. He only leads to victory!

Dear Heavenly Warrior, You are my Man of War. I lift my right hand out to You showing that by faith I choose to fight with You as You fight my enemies with Your mighty, outstretched right arm.

DAY 3: MIGHTY MAN

"The LORD will march out like a mighty man, like a warrior he will stir up his zeal; with a shout he will raise the battle cry and will triumph over his enemies."

ISAIAH 42:13

he Lord asked His servant in Isaiah 50:2b, "Was my arm too short to deliver you? Do I lack the strength to rescue you?" Are these the types of questions you have wondered concerning the Lord?

1. Jot down a few questions for the Lord you would love to have answers to.

Isaiah 59:1 says, "Surely the arm of the LORD is not too short to save, nor his ear too dull to hear" (Isaiah 59:1). Surely, you are not forgotten! The Lord really does hear you. The Lord really does want to save you. The Warrior really is strong enough. The Warrior really does love you.

Sister in the Lord, before God created the first man and woman, before Satan disguised himself as a serpent, and before Adam and Eve sinned, God had a plan for the world.

2. In the following verses underline the phrase that contains the reference to time.

   A. "For he chose us in him before the creation of the world to be holy and blameless in his sight. In love he predestined us for adoption of his glorious grace, which he has freely given us in the One he loves" (Ephesians 1:4-6).

   B. "But we should always give thanks to God for you, brethren beloved by the Lord has chosen you from the beginning through sanctification by the spirit and faith in the truth" (2 Thessalonians 2:13, NASB).

   C. "He has saved us and called us to a holy life—not because of anything we have done but because of his own purpose and grace. This grace was given us in Christ Jesus before the beginning of time, but is has now been revealed though the appearing of our Savior, Christ Jesus, who has destroyed death and has brought life and immortality to light through the gospel" (2 Timothy 1:9-10).

3. From the above verses, write what was God's plan before time even existed.

4. From the above verses, write how God planned to execute His plan of salvation.

5. From the previous verses, circle the word "grace."

Our mighty God had a marveling plan for each and every one of us which was accomplished through the cross of the Jesus Christ where we are made "holy and blameless," are adopted, "chosen," "saved," "called," and where we receive "sanctification," "life," and "immortality"! God's grace was manifested through His One and Only Son, Jesus Christ. We are the beneficiaries of His grace freely given, not through anything we could ever do for ourselves.

6. In the following verses, insert the word "grace" in the blanks provided.

"For the law was given through Moses; _____ and truth came through Jesus Christ" (John 1:17).

"Now I commit you to God and to the word of his _____, which can build you up and give you an inheritance among all those who are sanctified" (Acts 2:32).

"But the gift is not like the trespass. For if the many died by the trespass of the one man, how much more did God's _____ and the gift that came by the _____ of the one man, Jesus Christ, overflow to the many" (Romans 5:15)!

"For the _____ of God has appeared that offers salvation to all people" (Titus 2:11).

As the Scriptures testify, God's grace is sufficient for anyone who calls upon the Lord as their Savior. No one, not one is beyond the realm of His saving grace. Let us remember His grace richly given.

The prophet Isaiah prophesied the future plan of God that would bring salvation not just to God's people of the Old Testament but also to all the believers in Christ. Isaiah's prophecy is familiarly known as Jesus' birth announcement. Turn to Isaiah 9:6-7.

7. The referencing to the names of Jesus are described as His throne names. What are the four names prophesied in verse 6?

The beloved disciple, John, wrote of the Child who was prophesied to come as John was blessed to be one of the ones who walked the earth with Jesus. "In the beginning was the Word, and the Word was with God, and the Word was God. He was with God in the beginning" (John 1:1). "Word" is a name representing Jesus Christ. Jesus had been with God since the beginning and knew exactly the plan of His Father for salvation. John continues, "The Word became flesh and made his dwelling among us. We have seen his glory, the glory of the one and only Son, who came from the Father, full of grace and truth" (John 1:14). Jesus Himself proclaimed, "I and the Father are one" (John 10:30), and "Anyone who has seen me has seen the Father" (John 14:9b).

The Old Testament Mighty Warrior (Deuteronomy 3:24, Psalm 89:8, Zephaniah 3:17) is the same Mighty Warrior of the New Testament. "For in Christ all the fullness of the Deity lives in bodily form" (Colossians 2:9). Every divine attribute of the Father was in the person of Jesus Christ. Everything God the Father possessed, Jesus had at His disposal (Matthew 26:53).

Remember the second part of Nehemiah's charge to the Israelites as they faced enemies who wanted them dead as they were rebuilding the wall surrounding Jerusalem: "Remember the Lord" (Nehemiah 4:14)? One thing we should always remember especially in spiritual warfare is what our Mighty Warrior, Jesus Christ, defeated when He died and rose again.

Read Colossians 2:13-15.

Do you recognize the grace of God in verse 13? Even when we were sinners God saved us. It is truly unmerited favor—it is the biggest gift we could ever receive with absolutely no strings attached whatsoever. Paul wrote earlier in the letter, "For God was pleased to have all his fullness dwell in him and through him to reconcile to himself all things, whether things on earth or things in heaven, by making peace through his blood, shed on the cross" (Colossians 1:19-20). It was God's pleasure to free us from our sins through His only Son. This concept of sacrificing an only child for the sake of others is a difficult one for us to grasp. For now we only know in part, but will fully know when we see God face to face (1 Corinthians 13:12).

Colossians 2:15 reveals what He did to the demonic powers who had nothing more in mind than to keep Him behind the stone in the grave—dead.

8. Second Timothy 1:10 exposed that God destroyed what on the cross?

The *Message* Bible translates Colossians 2:15 in this way: "He stripped all the spiritual tyrants in the universe of their sham authority at the Cross and marched them naked through the streets."

9. In the space below write out Jesus' words in response to John's shock of seeing Him in his vision from Revelation 1:18.

Kay Arthur explains Colossians 2: 13-15: "O Beloved, do you see it? Not only did Jesus pay for your sins in full but He also triumphed over Satan and all his demonic rulers and authorities. The enemy is defeated . . . and he knows it."[18] It isn't a secret that Jesus forgives our sins and disarmed the powers of death. We need not be afraid of demonic powers—Jesus holds the "keys of death and Hades." We will live eternally with our Mighty Warrior in heaven. Jesus is coming back for us. I love the words Jesus spoke to the ones who arrested Him: "But I say to all of you: From now on you will see the Son of Man sitting at the right hand of the Mighty One and coming on the clouds of heaven" (Matthew 26:64).

On the fourth blank of your shield write: "I will remember the work on the cross."

⬧

Dear Heavenly Father, You are the LORD my God and You are with me. You are the Mighty Warrior who saves me. You take great delight in me and rejoice over me with singing. (Taken from Zephaniah 3:17.)

DAY 4: BEFORE YOUR PEOPLE

"When you, God, went out before your people, when you marched through the wilderness."

PSALM 68:7

ne of my most favorite attributes of God is His sovereignty. He is on the throne and in control at all times. He is all-powerful (1 Chronicles 29:10-13), all-knowing (Psalm 139:1-6), and all-present (Psalm 139:7-12). He is "the Lord God Almighty, who was, and is, and is to come" (Revelation 4:8). He knew us before we were even in the womb (Jeremiah 1:5); He is with us today (Psalm 46:1); and He knows our future (Jeremiah 29:11). I marvel that He knows and is aware of all concerning you and me, and yet He is with us in this exact moment. He isn't too big to be with you and me right now. He isn't too hurried to be with you and me right now. He isn't hidden in the past that He can't be with you and me right now. Marvelous! It is awesome how He can be omnipresent (all-present) and omniscient (all-knowing) at the same time. We desperately need Him to be, do we not?

1. What do you marvel at regarding God's ability to be all-knowing, all-powerful, and all-present?

Here is another theological word: *theocracy*. This term refers to the type of government the Old Testament believers had as God (*theo*) who was their authority and ruler (*cracy*). God led His people as King through the prophets of Moses and Aaron, but during the time of Samuel, the people rebelled and wanted an earthly king (1 Samuel 8). Even though the Lord fulfilled their fleshly demand, Samuel made sure they knew who their divine King still was (1 Samuel 12:14-15).

2. What was it exactly the people wanted an earthly king to do, according to 1 Samuel 8:19-20?

3. What specific reason did the people give as to why they demanded an earthly king?

These "other nations" were the pagan nations; ones who didn't have a covenant with the one, true God. They were the nations that God's people were not to learn from or be like (Deuteronomy 18:9). If anything, it should have been the direct opposite; the other nations should have desired Yahweh God to be their King because of the good things they saw from the believing nation.

If only God's people would have remembered the Lord! Had they, they would have recounted God as Mighty Warrior.

4. From the following verses, write out our Warrior's position.

Exodus 14:13-14

Deuteronomy 1:32-33

Deuteronomy 9:3

Deuteronomy 33:26

Joel 2:11

Psalm 68:6-7

Just because we cannot see Him, does not mean He isn't doing anything. Warrioress, God goes before you as your King to defeat your enemies and lead you to victory. Our responsibility is to surrender our will, submit to Him, and allow Him to take the lead. It isn't our job to take matters into our hands nor to be hasty and do or say something we may regret. Take what someone said to you or of you to the Lord. Take what someone did to you or didn't do to the Lord. Allow the omnipotent, omniscient, and omnipresent King to go before you with His mighty right arm to fight oppression and anything that attempts to keep you from accomplishing God's will for your life. Your very life matters. You have a purpose on this planet that only you can fulfill. Reject the lies that tell you otherwise. Surrender to the King of kings and Lord of lords.

Yesterday's lesson ended with a proclamation from the mouth of Jesus toward those who had Him arrested. He knew His life wasn't really in the hands of those who wanted Him dead. He knew His resurrection day was coming and that He would return to His Father's side and eventually come back in the clouds to receive His own (Matthew 26:64). The Day of the Lord has yet to come (1 Thessalonians 4:13-18), but we can know what we can expect to see and partake of thanks to the apostle John who obediently wrote down the vision given to him. Just before John adds to his writing, a great multitude breaks out in a shout, "Hallelujah! For our Lord God Almighty reigns. Let us rejoice and be glad and give him glory! For the wedding of the Lamb has come, and his bride has made herself ready. Fine linen, bright and clean, was given her to wear" (Revelation 19:6b-8). The "wedding of the Lamb" is called by theologians the eschatological Messianic banquet which will occur after the second coming of Christ. Jesus speaks of this even in Matthew 8:11, "I say to you that many will come from the east and the west, and will take their places at the feast with Abraham, Isaac, and Jacob in the kingdom of heaven." The prophet Isaiah also foretold of this same banquet as well as the great things about being in heaven: "On this mountain the LORD Almighty will prepare a feast of rich food for all peoples, a banquet of aged wine—the best of meats and the finest of wines. On this mountain he will destroy the shroud that enfolds all peoples, the sheet that covers all nations; he will swallow up death forever. The Sovereign LORD will wipe away the tears from all faces; he will remove his people's disgrace from all the earth. the LORD has spoken" (Isaiah 25:6-8). If you have yet to put your trust in the Lord and are not sure if you will be attending the wedding supper of the Lamb, then in just 3 simple steps you can know. All you have to remember is A-B-C. *A* is for *admit* that you are a sinner (Romans 3:23). *B* is for *believe* in the Lord Jesus as your Savior (Acts 13:31). And, *C* is for *confess* and your sins and repent (1 John 1:9). Openly talk aloud to God in these moments and know with certainty that you are adopted into His royal family. It is also a good idea to discuss your decision with a minister of a local church.

Please read slowly and carefully Revelation 19:11-16 and answer the following questions.

5. Where did these events take place (verse 11)?

6. What does the rider of the white horse do (verse 11)?

7. How is this rider dressed (verse 13)?

8. What is the rider's name (verse 13)?

9. Who were following him (verse 14)?

10. What were those following him wearing (verse 14)?

11. What comes out of his mouth (verse 15)?

From these passages we can conclude along with the theologians that this is a picture of our Mighty Warrior, Jesus Christ who is the rider of the white horse who will come to our rescue and take us home to be with Him forever and ever. Verse 14 tells us that the "armies of heaven were following him." Let's look at more Scriptures noting His army.

12. What do the following verses reveal about God's army?

Isaiah 13:4-5

Joel 2:11

Psalm 68:17-18

Revelation 17:14

Take comfort in the Warrior who goes before you leading an army too many to count who wars against evil and who will one soon day come and get His bride. May we be found ready.

Dear Heavenly Father, I truly want it said of me that I am one of Your called, chosen, and faithful followers. I believe Your team wins in the end, and I join You fighting for Your Kingdom.

Day 5: Refuge

"The Lord is a refuge for the oppressed, a stronghold in times of trouble."

PSALM 9:9

For the past nine days we have been studying the importance of spending time with God developing a personal relationship with Him so that throughout our days, months, and years we have something to remember. Remembering is a powerful weapon against the feelings of hopelessness and despair or any lie telling us we are alone. Recalling God's attributes and actions diffuses doubt and awakens hope to anyone who is remotely aware of his or her dependence upon God and His capabilities for those who call upon His name. Not only that, we got to study Scriptures that showcased the strength of the One who calls us by name, our "great and glorious" Lord.

1. Specifically, how have you benefitted from studying and practicing remembering the Lord?

Let's turn our attention to Psalm 77.

2. Why did the psalmist cry out to God?

3. What could the psalmist not do?

4. What did he doubt concerning God?

5. The turn in the psalm comes in verse 10. How are his thoughts different from the first nine verses?

6. Which hand of the Lord does he appeal to? Why?

7. According to verses 13-15, does the psalmist seem to doubt? Why or why not?

8. Do you know the story the psalmist is remembering in verses 16-20?

Don't you just love it?! A good story—miraculous at that—never gets old! The story of God parting the Red Sea for the Israelites as they were freed from Egyptian slavery and taken to the Promised Land was what the psalmist was reminiscing. What a day that must have been! They all knew it was God who had parted the waters and not some scientific explanation. It was obvious no one or no thing could have accomplished such a mind-blowing feat. Even the waters recognized their Creator!

9. What did the psalmist give as a reason the waters parted in verse 16?

10. So, the people and His creation knew it was God who performed the miracle of the dry land in the Red Sea, and yet what was not seen according to verse 19?

11. His feet did what, though in verse 20?

There He is again—going before His people, leading them to nothing but pure victory. It was like the psalmist expected to see God in the flesh going before them; he thought there would be literal footprints in the sand. His presence was so evident and undeniable, he imagined divine footprints to appear.

12. Have you had a mind-blowing experience with God that you knew beyond a shadow of doubt that God had been in your midst? Describe the circumstance and how you knew it could only have been God.

13. From the following verses, what type of situation is the person of God in and how is he kept safe?

	Situation	Safety
Deuteronomy 33:26-27		
2 Samuel 22:1-4		
Psalm 3:1-3		
Psalm 91:1-4		
Psalm 57:1		

He is our Refuge, our Shield, our Protector, our Defender!

In my opinion, no one knew this to be truer than Corrie Ten Boom. As a survivor of the Holocaust, she recalled: "'He who dwells in the shelter of the Most High will rest in the shadow of the Almighty' (Psalm 91:1). Now the message was clear. Although there was no light to guide me, I was still in God's will. Actually, when one is resting (abiding) under the shadow of the Almighty there will be no light, but that is because God's Presence is so near"[19]

It doesn't have to be only in the catastrophic times of life that we find our refuge in God. Personally, I need a safe haven on a daily basis. It is different than my normal devotional time; it is a place of rest and quietness. I discovered about myself that I use my back porch as a refuge. It is where I go when I need silence—a reprieve from the voices of the TV, radio, computer, work, and even family. It is where I go to hear the sound of nature: birds tweeting, wind whistling, children playing, and dogs barking. It is where I go to see the beauty of God's creation: birds flying to feed their young, leaves on trees swaying, freshly mown grass, dogs chasing balls, and children climbing trees. It is where I go to clear my head and unwind from the day's busy and crowded moments. It is where I go to feel the sun warming my tired body, or to hide in the shade to receive the coolness as it refreshes me. It is where I go to feel God's caring and tenderness toward me. He is sufficient and His goodness never ends!

As we conclude our two weeks on remembering the Lord, let's think about the times we especially need to remember Him.

14. In the blanks write the words, "I will remember."

When I need a refuge ___ _____ _____ the Lord.

When I am scared ___ _____ _____ the Lord.

When I feel weak ___ _____ _____ the Lord.

When I am confused ___ _____ _____ the Lord.

Now you write a time when you know you need to remember the Lord.

When _____ I will remember the Lord.

On the fifth blank of your shield, write the phrase: "I will remember the Lord who goes before me."

Dear Heavenly Father, "Be my rock of refuge, to which I can always go; give the command to save me, for you are my rock and my fortress" (Psalm 71:3).

PART 3:
AND FIGHT

———— ⚜ ————

For the last 10 days of our study we will concentrate on the more practical and applicable tactics of spiritual warfare. Nehemiah 4:14 has provided the direction of our time in God's Word. We will get to view it in its context as well as other short narratives of the Old Testament that teach us of the victories God gave to His people when they cooperated with Him. You can expect to learn of our spiritual weapons and how when used combat temptations, lies, oppositions, and other things the enemy throws our way to intimidate, seduce, belittle, thwart, or attack with the intention of eliminating us from fulfilling our callings. As you "fight" please keep in the forefront of your mind the very ones you are fighting for: daughters, sons, husbands, brothers, sisters, loved ones, and home.

Day 1: Wage War

"For though we live in the world, we do not wage war as the world does."

2 Corinthians 10:3

We have finally arrived at the most active part of the Bible study—the fighting. By now you should be able to recognize Satan's schemes of deception even though he hides behind a mask of seemingly harmless agendas. Understanding and discerning our real enemy is the first step as we prepare for battle. Acknowledging the enemy as the enemy positions us as believers on the winning side; we cannot lose being on the Mighty Warrior's team. It is absolutely imperative that our focus is on the instigator and author of the destruction, sin, and temptations in our lives and not directly on a person or thing. By no means are we crediting Satan with all means of temptations as our own flesh can be drawn to what is evil. The point is that as we actively engage in spiritual warfare, our target is the crafty ways Satan worms his way into particular areas of our lives. As we have studied previously, Paul made it clear that we are not fighting against "flesh and blood," but against "spiritual forces of evil in the heavenly realms" (Ephesians 6:12). Another point to note is that we are targeting the source of the manifestations of evil. We are attacking the cause, not the symptoms. For instance, if someone has a lung disease that produces coughing, treating the cough would be only a tiny part of a remedy because the cough would persist without the underlying problem being treated. Curing the lung disease would then consequentially eradicate the cough.

We have learned that the Old Testament warriors fought physically against their foes, and New Testament warriors fight spiritually as a direct benefit of Jesus as our sacrificial Lamb. Even though our battle is not in hand-to-hand combat, does not mean that we don't do anything physical. For example, when a new believer accepts Jesus as his or her Savior by inviting Jesus into his or her heart, this is no doubt a definite spiritual act. By faith we believe the Holy Spirit has made His residence within the believer even though we cannot see Him with our natural eyes. So, as a physical manifestation or expression of what happened on the inside of one's heart, one follows Jesus' example of baptism (Matthew 3:13-17). The immersion into the baptismal waters is symbolic of the death, burial, and resurrection of Jesus Christ. Baptism symbolizes to the observers that the one being baptized has given his or her life to the lordship of Jesus; it is an outward expression of what has happened inwardly. Physically, one gets into the water, goes under the water, and comes up out of the water. Baptism is a beautiful expression of what has already taken place in the heart of the believer. The next 10 days will provide opportunities for us to outwardly express what God has done, is doing, and what we believe by faith He can do supernaturally.

When I reference "fight" as coming from when Nehemiah charged the Israelites as they were doing the very thing God ordained and equipped them to do—build the wall around Jerusalem—I am referring to very things God has called you and I to do as daughters of the King. The things we are called to do are the very things that Satan wants to thwart. The apostle Paul speaks plainly when he states, "We have different gifts, according to the grace given to each of us. If your gift is prophesying, then prophesy in accordance with your faith; if it is serving, then serve; if it is teaching, then teach; if it is to encourage, then give encouragement; if it is giving, then give generously; if it is to lead, do it diligently; if it is to show mercy, do it cheerfully" (Romans 12:6-8). Of course, this verse is not the entirety of what God has called us to do. His Word is full of commandments that when obeyed produce many blessings.

1. What identical words does Paul have for Timothy as they spread the gospel together in 1 Timothy 1:18-19 and 1 Timothy 6:12?

As Paul prepared for the end of his life, he wrote to Timothy and told him that he had done just what he had expected from Timothy. Paul's conscience was clear, and with deep conviction and a sigh of relief he wrote, "I have fought the good fight, I have finished the race, I have kept the faith" (2 Timothy 4:7).

Life in Christ is oh so good, *not* oh so easy. Those words uttered by Paul in 2 Timothy did not come onto the page without trouble and heartache and near death experiences. He fought, he finished, and he held on to his faith in the midst of unimaginable confrontations.

2. List all the extremes Paul lived through as recorded in 2 Corinthians 11:23-28.

Paul is like a protagonist in a fictional thriller than goes up against the most threatening, dangerous, and horrific situations and comes out as the one who never dies. If Paul's life had been a non-fiction movie, we would have walked away exclaiming that that would never happen in real life; no one could outlive all he went through! He did survive, and dear one, you will too.

Life is serious business, and in some seasons, it may be scarce of humor. To laugh may seem more like a luxury reserved for those who appear to not have a care in the world. The dark seasons have their way of shading the light even when we needed it the most. Life in Christ is a fight, but it is also a battle to be won!

Our battles are won with the weapons God has generously supplied. "His divine power has given us everything we need for a godly life through our knowledge of him who called us by his own glory and goodness" (2 Peter 1:3).

3. According to 2 Corinthians 10:4, our weapons are not what?

4. What are our weapons?

5. What is the purpose of the weapons?

In 2 Peter 1:3 and in 2 Corinthians 10:4, Paul acknowledges that God's "divine power" is the supernatural force behind his ability to fight and to keep the faith. It is Christ in us that gives us exactly what we need at the exact time we need it.

Read 2 Corinthians 10: 3-6 from *The Message:*

"The world is unprincipled. It's dog-eat-dog out there! The world doesn't fight fair. But we don't live or fight our battles that way—never have and never will. The tools of our trade aren't for marketing or manipulation, but they are for demolishing that entire massively corrupt culture. We use our powerful God-tools for smashing warped philosophies, tearing down barriers erected against the truth of God, fitting every loose thought and emotion and impulse into the structure of life shaped by Christ. Our tools are ready at hand for clearing the ground of every obstruction and building lives of obedience into maturity."

6. Underline the portion of the Scripture that resonates the most to you.

7. Why did you underline that portion?

We do live in a "dog-eat-dog" world. Seems people are taking anyone and everyone and their dog to court. Seems no one is who he or she claims to be. Seems like we are one generation away from a godless generation. Seems like absolutes is a thing of the past. But . . . God has a plan.

Dear Heavenly Father, You have generously supplied me with spiritual tools that I can practically use against the enemy who opposes Your will. Thank You for leading me to victory.

DAY 2: SETTING OUT

"The blast will be the signal for setting out."

NUMBERS 10:6b

*E*xcuses. Rationales. Justifications. Anything to get out of doing something we don't want to do or we don't feel like doing. We want someone else to do it. We are spoiled, and we like it that way. Are you going into battle and fight? Or are you going to pretend the matter will take care of itself? Or are you going to ignore it hoping no one notices? Or are you going to complain about it to your friends and even your pastor? Or are you going to become depressed about the situation and sleep or eat it away?

1. What keeps you from fighting?

Get out of bed! Off the couch! Away from the computer! Put your phone down! There is a war to be waged and you have a responsibility to the kingdom of God.

The rich history of the Israelites in the Old Testament has proven to portray extraordinary illustrations of God and His divine role of a Warrior King leading His people in and throughout battles (Romans 15:4). This history provides insights into our own battles in the 21st century; it sets up precedence to fuel our faith to get up and fight.

In today's age, we cannot fathom life without mobile phones. We almost have too many ways of "getting the word out." For instance, my daughters' schools send information about one particular thing via phone call, text message, voice activated email, several types of social media, school website, school enewsletter, and, of course, word-of-mouth. Sometimes, I just want to scream, "I got it the first time!"

Let's turn our attention to the instructions God gave to Moses regarding the methods of communication between Moses and the people. In Moses' time, they got one shot to get the information out to the people. Read Numbers 10:1-10.

2. What was the means of communication (verse 2)?

3. Who were involved and what were they to do when they heard the two trumpets (verse 3-4)?

4. When the troops were gathered, what was the signal for "setting out" (verse 6)?

5. The blowing of the trumpets served as what (verse 8)?

6. When and why were the priests to blow the trumpets (verse 9)?

7. What is the significance of the sound of the trumpet (verse 10)?

8. From your memory of what we studied in Part 2, why do you think God established the Israelite tradition of blowing the trumpets as an act of remembering?

God didn't want them to forget what He had done for them by providing and protecting them. He desired that it get passed down to each generation to know God and His deeds, which ultimately revealed His love for them. They didn't have access to pen and paper to keep a record of their journeys with God. They didn't have scrapbooks to display the events of the past. They didn't have blogs or websites to publish the works they saw the Lord do. The things God's people witnessed were solely communicated orally.

Have you ever noticed how important sounds are to God? Sounds, followed by extremely significant actions, occur throughout the Bible.

10. Write what noise was heard and the action that took place from the following verses.

	Noise	Action
Joshua 6:20		
Judges 7:22		
2 Samuel 5:24		
Psalm 47:5		
Isaiah 6:4		
Luke 1:44		
Acts 2:4-6		

As you saw from the above verses, God intervened when He heard the sound of trumpets, the sound of shouts, and the sound of voices. Obviously, when we want God to intervene or our friends to help us, we are not going to literally blow on a trumpet. The trumpet was the vehicle to alert God and for His people to come together in battle. It is actually more than that though. I am convinced that the sounds alerted more than just God and man; it resounded into the heavenlies. The armies of heaven and the demons of hell were alerted too of the signal for war. "For our struggle is not against flesh and blood, but against the rulers, against the authorities, against the powers of this dark world and against the spiritual forces of evil in the heavenly realms" (Ephesians 6:12).

The sound of our voices with the Spirit of the living God residing in us and with the authority He has given us is the most powerful weapon we possess. Speaking the name of Jesus and crying out to God sends demons away and angels to our side (Acts 16:18; 12:11). The speaking of the name of Jesus out loud is the outward expression of what our heart's are crying out. Don't be silent. Opportunities that supply time for you to be alone, use it to speak the name of Jesus into the heavenlies.

First things first: If we are going into battle, it has to be one in which God initiates and leads. Just as Moses did not want to proceed anywhere without God's presence, so it is with us (Exodus 33:15). We may not have a trumpet to sound, but we do have an invitation from God Almighty to use our voices to call upon Him.

11. From the following verses write what happens when we call upon our God.

Jeremiah 33:3

Psalm 3:4

Psalm 18:3, 6

Psalm 50:15

Romans 10:13

Speaking the name of Jesus in a whisper or a shout as a prayer testifies that you need Him and have faith in Him a little or a lot. Crying out to Jesus is a weapon that cuts through the pain, the heaviness, the heartache, the loneliness, and the depths of despair. Crying out to Jesus is a weapon that gives back strength, hope, authority, peace, and lifts our heads.

12. Look again at Psalm 18. David wrote this after God rescued him from his worst enemy. Who is God to David in verse 2? List every description David gives.

Sounds like the exact Warrior King we have been studying! God is so faithful. Can you feel the intimacy David experienced with God during the heat of battle? David acknowledged God was the One who preserved his life even though David himself was known to slay "tens of thousands" (1 Samuel 18:7). David was a commander in King Saul's army, but when David had bigger and better victories (because the Lord was with David and no longer with Saul), Saul became so jealous that he wanted David dead. When David became aware of the plot Saul had on his life, he spent years wandering from place to place because Saul and his men continued to hunt him down. David feared for his life every day for years. He had already been anointed by Samuel to the next king of Israel, but his life resembled more of a criminal's life than a soon to be king. (The accounts of David running and hiding from Saul can be found in 1 Samuel 18-31.) David penned the words to Psalm 18 in utter relief from the life of running and being hunted. He testified to what the Warrior King can and will do for one man who cries out to God for help.

13. Reread Psalm 18:4-5. What entangles you? What overwhelms you? What coils around you? Who or what confronts you?

Reach up your hand to your omnipotent Warrior King. See the look in His eyes as they are on you, His child. His arms are mighty and ready for you. Nothing is impossible with Him. Let Him embrace you.

"He reached down on high and took hold of me; he drew me out of deep waters. He rescued me from my powerful enemy, from my foes who were too strong for me" (Psalm 18:16-17).

He can take care of you. God really can do something for even you. His plans will work for you. You are not the one person that cannot be helped. This situation you are in is His business. He is in the marriage business. He is in the money business. He is in the health business. He is in the church business. He is in the car business, restaurant business, insurance business, political business. Your business is God's business. There is nothing He cannot handle. It is all His turf. Open your mouth and cry out to Jesus today. "Shout it aloud, do not hold back. Raise your voice like a trumpet" (Isaiah 58:1a).

On the sixth blank of your shield write: "I will call upon the name of Jesus."

Dear Heavenly Father, I cry out to You. I have nowhere else to turn; You are it. I need You. I want You. Send Your angels to minister to me. Thank You for being my Rescuer, my Deliverer, my Rock, my Fortress, my Shield, and my King.

DAY 3: WHEN THE DAY

"Therefore put on the full armor of God, so that when the day of evil comes, you may be able to stand your ground, and after you have done everything, to stand."

*P*lanning vacations can take lots of time. Deciding on a desired location that the whole family can agree on can take months in itself. Seriously, so much planning goes into getting away for a weekend or a week-long vacation. There is so much to plan ahead from the places to stay, food, clothes to pack, recreation, and transportation. Then, you have to think about the pets left at the house, who's getting the mail and watering the flowers, getting off from work, and so forth. But, we take the time to plan because we know that an adventure awaits at our vacation destination. Even if we don't get to go on a vacation any time soon, we still like to plan a vacation spot for the "one day" we hope to go.

One thing most Americans don't tend to plan for is the day when "the day of evil comes" (Ephesians 6:13). It is certainly something we would never daydream about or wish for when we blow out our birthday candles. The day of evil, unfortunately, comes. We never want it to come, we never wish it to come, but still it comes.

The writer of the book of Ephesians, the apostle Paul, worded this sentence as "when the day of evil comes," not *if* or *maybe*, or *possibly*, but "when." He was serious when he admonished them to be prepared. Paul's words also serve as a warning to us. "What is the day of evil?" you may ask. Is it the news we read about in the local paper? Is it the news we hear on the national news? Is it the day when the anti-christ comes? Is it personal? Is it corporate? Is it a literal day, or is it used metaphorically?

I am convinced that the day of evil is all of the above. I am even more convinced as Paul directed the letter to the church of Ephesus that the day of evil should be taken personally since he went on to explain the individual pieces of spiritual armor supplied to bring victory against the evil one (Ephesians 6:13-18). Obviously, armor is what a warrior wore in the Old Testament as he fought in hand-to-hand combat. Paul speaks of the spiritual armor one wears as spiritual protection whether defensively or offensively. Paul is giving us a word picture to help us understand and apply the spiritual weapons of warfare against evil. John reminds the believers that "whole world is under the control of the evil one" (1 John 5:19). In the very next verse he emphasizes that those who know Him "are in him who is true by being in his Son Jesus Christ" (1 John 5:20). We have assurance as believers that even though evil is prevalent personally and/or corporately, we are in Christ who has already triumphed over sin and death. Nothing we go through in our day of evil is too hard for our Warrior King!

Read Ephesians 6:10-13.

1. The armor of God is meant to go up against what?

This isn't pretend play like we did when we were young or like our children do today. The armor of God is very real in the heavenly realm; it is evident to angels and demons whether we have it on or not. We have faith to believe we are wearing spiritual armor even though we cannot see it in the physical. Paul isn't making a suggestion like a physician suggests wearing a helmet when riding a bike. Paul is addressing a serious matter with the church and orders them to get dressed spiritually for a very good reason.

2. What is coming according to Ephesians 6:13?

3. With armor on, what is the first thing we are to do?

The word *stand* can be applied literally or figuratively. In the literal it means to stand on your feet. It means to get up. It means to not sit or lie down. It means to establish your ground; to put your feet on solid ground and to be ready. Figuratively it means to not be afraid of your enemy. It means to not let the fear of the unknown stop you. It means to know who you are in Christ. It means to not run away, hide, or cower. Whether literally or figuratively to "stand" means to prepare yourself, to get into position. It also means to hold up to what you know to be the truth. To the church in Thessalonica, Paul exhorted the church to do both "stand" and "hold on," "Therefore, brothers and sisters, stand firm and hold on to the traditions that we taught you, whether by speech or by letter (2 Thessalonians 2:15, NET). I don't know about you, but sometimes, I just have to get up on my feet and prove my faith. Courageous acts of getting out of bed and off the couch to do something exemplifies my faith whether it be as simple as making dinner or as profound as facilitating a Bible study. James adds, "In the same way, faith by itself, if it is not accompanied by action, is dead" (James 2:17).

One of my all-time favorite chapters in the Old Testament is found tucked away in the latter part of the history of the Israelites, which was retold to the generations following the Babylonian captivity. Second Chronicles 20 recounts one of the greatest and longest days known to Jehoshaphat, King of Judah. We will not read the entire chapter today, but we will come back several times to this chapter over the course of the next two weeks. (Yes, it is that good!)

For now, please read 2 Chronicles 20:1-5.

1. What was the bad news told to Jehoshaphat?

2. How do we know that this was a surprise attack?

In chapter 17, we learn that Jehoshaphat's "heart was devoted to the ways of the LORD" (verse 6), and that the surrounding lands feared him so much so that they did not war against him. Chapter 19 is a report of Jehoshaphat working diligently appointing judges to govern all the peoples of Judah. Then, out of nowhere, when Jehoshaphat was doing the work of the Lord, news of the enemy waging war frightened him to the core of his soul. Jehoshaphat's day of evil came when he heard: "A vast army is coming against you." An enemy that is larger and stronger and prepared to destroy him and his people were well on their way.

3. According to verse 3, what were Jehoshaphat's first two courses of action after hearing the report?

4. What did the people of Judah do?

Jehoshaphat and the people of Judah did not blame God for the vast army, nor did they run and hide.

5. What is another response Jehoshaphat and the people could have done in response to the report?

May our first response not be to blame, retreat, or call upon another person, but to call out to our God, Jesus Christ.

6. According to verse 5, what is the action verb?

It takes courage to face your worst enemy. It takes courage to lead your family. It takes courage to do something. It takes courage to stand.

7. Turn again to Ephesians 6:10-14. How many times does the word *stand* appear?

The significance of choosing to stand and face opposition is huge. It cannot be overlooked. No matter your fears, no matter how hopeless it seems, no matter how incapable you feel, just stand! Standing is a weapon of spiritual warfare that cuts through mediocrity, laziness, slothfulness, apathy, and passivity. Standing is a weapon that gives back dignity, authority, humility, and power to resist the evil one. We stand abandoned, completely surrendered to all of who God is—the living God full of truth, wisdom, and power.

Going back to 2 Chronicles 20, read what Jehoshaphat prayed aloud in verses 6-9.

8. Verses 6-7 are a reminder of whom and what?

9. Verse 9 proclaims that the people have already promised to do what two actions?

10. What two things are they counting on God to do?

11. Read verses 10-11. In your own words, of what is Jehoshaphat reminding God?

In our situations, we may remind God that He is the One who gave us the child(ren). We may remind Him that He gave us the job. We may remind Him of the vow we took with our husband. We have permission to look back on how it all began and remind God of past obedience, and that the current situation doesn't make any sense.

Read the surrender statement in verse 12. This is a cry for help. The psalmist, too, looked up for help, "I lift up my eyes to the mountains—where does my help come from? My help comes from the LORD, the Maker of heaven and earth" (Psalm 121:1-2).

Read 2 Chronicles 20:13. Jehoshaphat gathered the people together after the bad report, stood, and prayed aloud. No one had a clue what to do about the vast army. Jehoshaphat got an army of civilians together—the dads, moms, grandfathers, grandmothers, and not to be left out, the "little ones." Just regular people going about a regular day in need of an extraordinary miracle. Whole families left their homes, came to the temple, gathered as a community, and "stood there before the LORD."

Can you picture it with me? Families standing, feeling completely helpless, with their faces to the sky and their eyes on the Maker of heaven and earth. They were not budging until they heard from their Warrior King. They were not going anywhere until they got an answer from their Commander of the Kingdom of God. I wish Scripture recorded how long they stood. Was it seconds? Minutes? Hours?

Time was ticking. The enemy was getting closer. Their very lives were at stake. What would God do for them this time? How were they to fight?

12. As they stood, the Spirit of the Lord fell on one young man, Jahaziel, who informed Jehoshaphat and all the people what to do (verses 14-17). What were his instructions?

As you cry out to God, wait patiently for His answer, and know that it just may come through someone else.

On your seventh blank on your shield write: "I will stand."

Dear Heavenly Father, thank You for knowing what is unknown to me. Thank You that nothing takes You by surprise. I lift my head up and put my eyes on You. I choose to stand and wait patiently for Your answers.

DAY 4: CONSECRATE YOURSELVES

"Joshua told the people, Consecrate yourselves, for tomorrow the LORD will do amazing things among you"

JOSHUA 3:5

Yesterday's lesson took us to a gripping account in the Old Testament of what one man's leadership and dependence on God in the face of overwhelming circumstances can teach us in our own times of not knowing what to do. Today's study will spotlight another man of God who led God's people who, too, was in need of a miracle not because of who was attacking them, but because they were about to be the surprise attackers in the day of war. Jehoshaphat and the people found themselves on the defensive. Today our men find themselves on the offensive.

Days before the fulfillment of a long-awaited promise, God told Joshua the requirements and details for the Israelites to go to war and win the property known as the Promised Land, which was first promised to Abraham (Genesis 15). The possession of the land didn't come on a silver platter; it came by hand-to-hand combat. It came with courage and faith to believe God will be faithful to those who obey Him.

Please read Joshua 3:1-11.

1. What did Joshua and the Israelites do early in the morning (verse 1)?

2. When the Ark of the Covenant was being carried, what were the people to do (verse 3)?

The Ark of the Covenant was the sacred object that symbolized the presence of God. It was one of the pieces of furniture used in the tabernacle. It was the one piece that God manifested His glory to the high priest in the Most Holy Place as the high priest atoned for the sins of the people and himself (Exodus 25:10-22).

3. Where were the people to be positioned in respect to the Ark of the Covenant (verse 3)?

4. According to verses 9-11, what did their position behind the Ark of the Covenant symbolize?

5. Speaking of timing . . . before the people set foot in the waters of the Jordan, they had to do what according to verse 5?

6. What is the promise attached to the command?

The people were very familiar with the term *consecrate*; they knew exactly what needed to be accomplished the night before. They knew the drill and had high expectations of "the living God" who was among them (Joshua 3:10).

The consecration routine consisted of washing their clothes, having no sexual relations, abstaining from eating any creature that crawls or walks on all four of its feet, and other specifications (Exodus 19:10, 14-15; Leviticus 11:41-44). God declared to them the purpose of the consecration, "I am the Lord your God; consecrate yourselves and be holy, because I am holy" (Leviticus 11:44a).

The word *consecrate* in the King James Version is *sanctify* which means to pronounce ceremonially or morally clean. It also means to dedicate and to be holy. Joshua and the people were cognizant that this wasn't just a war they would go out and fight by their own strength, they very well knew that they were going to need the supernatural power of the Warrior King Himself. In modern times we may explain consecration something like this: "Get ready to see God do only what He can do"!

Jehoshaphat acknowledged that he needed God to do "amazing things" for His people which is why he immediately proclaimed a fast for not just himself but for all of Judah (2 Chronicles 20:3).

7. The Bible provides multiple examples of times of fasting. From the following verses record who fasted and why.

	Who	Why
1 Samuel 7:6		
Ezra 8:21-23		
Esther 4:16		
Matthew 4:1-2		
Acts 13:2-3		

I am sure you noticed the variety of reasons for fasting. Fasting is still very much a sharp weapon of spiritual warfare that cuts through dark places, hardness, sickness, strongholds, and demonic activity. It is a weapon that gives back health, clarity, holiness, purity, and angelic beings. It is a weapon that sets us apart to be a sanctified vessel open and emptied to be filled with God's goodness, righteousness, and holiness.

Don't let the convenience of foods and the accustomed lifestyles of regular eating stop you from this powerful and effective weapon. Do some research at a local library, bookstore, or on the Internet as resources for the right kind of fast for you. There are different kinds of fasts as well as lengths of fasts. Biblical fasts were as short as one day of daylight hours to as long as 40 days. A popular fast, which is adapted from Daniel 1:8-14 is when one consumes only whole grains, fruits, and vegetables for 10 days. I particularly love this fast because you still get to eat which makes it less awkward around friends, family, and co-workers. No one would even have to know you are on a fast.

8. How do Jesus' words about fasting in Matthew 6:16-18 encourage you?

During times of fasting, do not feel as if you have to go pray while every-one else is eating. By fasting, you are utilizing a spiritual weapon. When you do pray, then you are combining two very effective weapons simultaneously. "When you fast and pray in tandem, it's almost like a moving sidewalk that gets you to your desired destination in half the time. Fasting has a way of fast-tracking our prayers. Because fasting is harder than praying, fasting is a form of praying hard."[20]

Let's conclude by going back to Joshua to see how their long, momentous, and miraculous day ended. Read Joshua 3:14—4:7, 10-18.

9. What were the priests with the Ark of the Covenant doing in the middle of the Jordan as the people hurried over?

10. What was the purpose of collecting the stones from the middle of the Jordan (verses 4: 5-7)?

We will never know what story we will have to pass on to our children and grandchildren if we first don't decide to trust God and put our faith into action.

———————— ❈ ————————

Dear Heavenly Father, I comprehend that there is a battle waging, and I have a choice to be a part of it or not. I choose today to be Your warrioress.

Day 5: The Battle Is Not Yours

"This is what the LORD says to you, 'Do not be afraid or discouraged because of this vast army. For the battle is not yours, but God's.'"

2 CHRONICLES 20:15b

*L*et's continue our reading in 2 Chronicles 20. Remember we left off with the men, women, and "little ones" standing as God spoke through Jahaziel. But for the sake of review please read 2 Chronicles 20:1-13.

What a precious gift these parents gave their children. They taught the children that God is in control and He is their authority. They taught the children that He loves them and cares about them. They taught the children what to do in times of crises.

1. What do you think the children learned from this experience?

2. Did your parents teach you a spiritual lesson in the midst of tragedy, overwhelming situation, or crisis?

Now read the context of our theme verse in Nehemiah 4:1-14.

3. Who were the Israelites "vast army"/opposition/enemy as they worked on the wall of protection around their city (verses 1,7)?

4. What were their tactics of opposition (verses 1-2,8)?

5. How far were the enemies willing to go to stop the Israelites (verse 11)?

6. What did the Israelites, thanks to Nehemiah's leadership, do to "meet this threat" (verses 9, 13)?

Never underestimate your family, no matter your children's ages or younger brothers and sisters ages. In the fight for our homes, marriages, children, finances, relationships, jobs, health, and for our own sanity, getting your family involved for prayer and support and fasting is one of the best weapons to combat the enemy. Not all details have to be shared. Please use discernment and discretion in your honesty, but, by all means, get them on your side. King David, in praise to God, sung, "From the lips of children and infants you have ordained praise because of your enemies, to silence the foe and the avenger" (Psalm 8:2).

We are not really sure when or where or through whom opposition will come. Paul warns us that the day of evil will come. We have got to already be ready! We cannot afford to be ignorant. Nehemiah and all the men even took their weapons when they went for water (Nehemiah 4:23). Jehoshaphat received the bad news of the vast army on a regular work day. David's chief enemy was his best friend's dad and his father-in-law. Joshua and the Israelites enemies were living on their Promised Land. Jesus' betrayer was among His inner circle of the 12 disciples. Eve's deceiver showed up in the most unexpected place ever, the Garden of Eden.

Ultimately, the day of evil will come when the antichrist comes "in accordance with how Satan works. He will use all sorts of displays of power through signs and wonders that serve the lie, and all the ways that wickedness deceives those who are perishing" (2 Thessalonians 2:9-10). The spirit of the antichrist is already at work (2 Thessalonians 2:7). If we don't detect him at work now and arm ourselves now, how will we or our children and grandchildren be able to recognize the antichrist when he comes? John's words need to be announced: "Dear children, this is the last hour; and as you have heard that the antichrist is coming, even now many antichrists have come" (1 John 2:18).

Read 2 Chronicles 20:14-21. The Spirit of the LORD fell on Jahaziel and gave him the battle plan.

7. From verse 15, what was the first instruction told to the king and all the people?

Sounds familiar, huh? We really are scared people, too, for good reasons. Our enemy is very intimidating. We feel reduced to a helpless and sometimes paralyzed state of mind. Our strength drains from us like a mother who finds out her child has a terminal illness. Yes, we, too, are scared and horrified. I believe when God told His people to not be afraid, He wants us to not give in to fear, which could move us to not do anything. Don't let your fears stop you from facing your enemy. Remember who your God is. Remember what He has already done for you. He isn't going to stop loving you. He isn't going to stop caring for you. He is with you.

8. From the last part of verse 15, whom does Jahaziel say the battle belongs to?

He who has our hairs numbered (Matthew 10:30); He who tells us to cast our anxiety upon Him (1 Peter 5:7); He who admonishes us to put on His armor (Ephesians 6:11); He who gives us our very being (Acts 17:28); He who redeemed us from the power of Satan (Acts 26:18); He who died for us while we were still sinners (Romans 5:8); He who adopted us (Romans 8:15); He who forgives us (1 John 1:9); He who loves us (1 John 4:19); He who abides in us (John 15:5); He who is coming again (Revelation 22:20); will also be the One who fights for you (Exodus 14:4)!

Add your eighth tactic of your battle plan to your shield. Write: "God will fight for me!"

For our prayer today, let's pray Psalm 44:4-8: "You are my King and my God, who decrees victories for Jacob. Through you we push back our enemies; through your name we trample our foes. I put no trust in my bow, my sword does not bring me victory; but you give us victory over our enemies, you put our adversaries to shame. In God we make our boast all day long, and we will praise your name forever."

Day 1: Place Where You Stand Is Holy

"The commander of the Lord's army replied, 'Take off your sandals, for the place where you are standing is holy.' And Joshua did so."

Joshua 5:15

My hope in writing this study is that you have gained an education on the schemes of our archenemy, Satan, and that your spiritual eyes are opened a little wider to his activity in your personal life, life of your family, or the life of a loved one. By no means do I label myself an expert. I do believe I unknowingly made myself a target. I, like Eve, acknowledge that I was ingeniously deceived and that I participated in something outside of God's will. I can confidently state what Joseph lovingly responded to his brothers who sold him into slavery, "You intended to harm me, but God intended it for good" (Genesis 50:20). I didn't learn the material in this book by myself. By God's mercies, He surrounded me with godly women and men who loved me and saw beyond my destructive ways and guided me to walk in truth. I made a conscious decision to allow them to lead me as I trusted their direction to get me back to a place I could begin again trusting myself. It truly was a day-to-day journey of which I am thankful. My prayer is that my experience and the things I learned can prevent someone else from Satan's deception.

Crime experts have provided useful information to educate readers on personal safety. Some of the information includes being aware of your surroundings and paying attention to see if someone is following you whether in a vehicle or walking. Wearing headphones is not recommended while exercising outside because it prevents you from hearing someone approaching. Go with your instincts even if you embarrass yourself a little. Experts recommend making noise if someone does approach you or put his hands on you. It even wouldn't be too much to carry a whistle like on your key chain.

Just these four pieces of information can alone be very valuable in prevention of being a victim. I believe these can also be applied to the spiritual realm against an unseen enemy. Recognizing Satan's fingerprint in conversations, in the media, in entertainment, in behaviors, and in opportunities is what we need to be aware of. With the Holy Spirit residing in us, He can give us discernment to see through others and situations to direct us in decisions (John 14:26).

The advice to make noise makes me smile ☺. It makes me think about our lesson over the trumpet—shout, sound the alarm, cry out for help! We do not have to be alone in our struggles "because you know that your brothers throughout the world are undergoing the same kind of sufferings" (1 Peter 5:9b).

Keeping in mind our need for awareness of our surroundings in the natural as well as the supernatural realm for protection, let's revisit the Old Testament accounts we have been studying. Allow the Holy Spirit to teach you and to apply it to your current circumstances.

We learned in Joshua 3 about Joshua leading the Israelites to their Promised Land. They first had to do battle against the Jordan River before crossing over to their rightful territory, but not without another battle. Before advancing Joshua encountered a surprise visit from a heavenly being who was actually a manifestation of the presence of God which is presumed to be a pre-incarnate Jesus. Joshua got one of the few known visitations of God in bodily form before

Jesus was sent to earth born of a virgin. This visual appearance is known as a theophany. The heavenly being Joshua encountered was not God Himself as no one can see God and live (Exodus 33:20, 1 Timothy 6:16), but rather the "commander of the army of the Lord" who is revealed in Revelation 19:11 as Jesus. Please read Joshua's encounter before he was to advance his army to Jericho in Joshua 5:13-15.

1. What indicated to Joshua that this man was a man of war?

2. What was Joshua's first response when the angel of the Lord identified himself?

3. What was Joshua asked to do and why?

4. Who now is in charge of leading the battle at Jericho (from the heavenly position)?

Read 2 Chronicles 20:15-18.

5. To whom did the battle belong?

6. What were the people to do?

7. What did Jahaziel order the people to do?

8. In response to the prophetic words from Jahaziel, what did Jehoshaphat do?

9. How is his response similar to Joshua's in Joshua 5:14?

10. Read Nehemiah 4:6-13. What did Nehemiah have done to meet the threat of opposition?

The New Testament offers the spiritual application to the Old Testament accounts of God's men and women fighting for what is rightfully theirs—victory from the enemy!

Read James 4:7.

11. What is the first thing James instructs?

The word *submit* is a military term used to acknowledge hierarchy of those in command. The undeniably wonderful narratives of Joshua falling face down to the Commander of the army of the Lord , and Jehoshaphat falling face down before the Lord, and Nehemiah praying to God completely exemplifies what is meant for us to do in response to a threat. We are to come under the authority of our Lord and Savior, Jesus Christ. He will go before us and instruct us on our part.

12. What is the second instruction in James 4:7?

Get this: The term *resist* actually means to "stand against" in Greek. Joshua stood on holy ground. Jahaziel commanded the people of Judah to "Take up your positions; stand firm and see the deliverance the LORD will give you" (2 Chronicles 20:17). Nehemiah "posted a guard day and night" (Nehemiah 4:9) and posted them "by families, with their swords, spears, and bows" (4:13).

13. What is the promise when we resist the devil?

14. Then James tells us to do what in James 4:8?

And God will come near you! It is His battle anyway. It is He who defeated the enemy and every opposing force with the finished work on the cross. Colossians 2:13b-15 says, "He forgave us all our sins, having canceled the charge of our legal indebtedness, which stood against us and condemned us; he has taken it away, nailing it to the cross. And having disarmed the powers and authorities, he made a public spectacle of them, triumphing over them by the cross." Jesus Christ did all of this for you. Let Him continue to put His fingerprints in your conversations, in your media, in your entertainment, in your behaviors, and in your opportunities. "God is light; in him there is no darkness at all" (1 John 1:5).

For the ninth blank on your shield, write: "I will submit to my Lord."

Dear Heavenly Father, As Moses cried out to you in desperation, I too exalt "show me your glory" (Exodus 33:18). My battle is Your battle. I submit myself to You and acknowledge You as my authority.

DAY 2: ARMOR OF LIGHT

"The night is nearly over; the day almost here. So let us put aside the deeds of darkness and put on the armor of light."

ROMANS 13:12

Hands down, the most popular New Year's resolution is to lose weight and eat healthier. Gym memberships increase at the first of the year, and marketers promote fitness, targeting this huge population of Americans trying to achieve their New Year's goals. We need all the motivation we can get, huh? Most of the time, we do not feel like exercising because it would most likely mean we need to get up early or get home later in the evenings. We like the results exercise provides, but more times than not, it seems too burdensome to get started.

One of my motivations genuinely happens to be the wardrobe. After coming home from work and changing into my work out clothes, I feel more impelled to get my work out in! Fitness clothes are so fashionable and functional; who wouldn't be inspired from wearing them? It isn't just the cuteness of the fitness fashion; there is a mind-set change with the actual taking off work clothes and switching to work out clothes. My mind goes into another gear. I may have been mentally exhausted returning home from work, but the literal changing of the clothes refreshes me and gives me a new energy.

If there is mental power associated with the changing of clothes, imagine the supernatural power from above that is ours when we choose by an act of our will (not emotions) as we "put on the full armor of God" (Ephesians 6:11a)?

Read Ephesians 6:10-13.

1. According to verse 10, on whose strength do we rely?

Fierce Warrioress, you don't have it in you to be strong enough. Your strength isn't enough for the battle; you can't do it. Stop convincing yourself otherwise. Don't believe the lies that if you just do this or that that everything will be all right. It is time to surrender our will for God's; our armor for God's armor.

Ephesians 6:11 tells us the only way to take our stand in the spiritual battle is with God's full armor. What you are going through or have gone through or will go through is a spiritual battle between the kingdom of darkness and the kingdom of light. Our spiritual weapons are used to defeat evil forces that originate from Satan's demise. We are called to fight in a battle that is of our heavenly citizenship, not our earthly citizenship. We have a higher purpose. We are not of this world just as Jesus was not (John 17:16; Philippians 3:20).

Nothing is hidden from our Lord and Savior, Jesus Christ. "He reveals the deep things of darkness and brings deep shadows into the light" (Job 12:22). His divine weapons subdue everything. His light is mightier than the deepest, darkest secret; than the toughest, strongest addiction; than the scariest, direst abuse; and than the harshest, hardest heart.

Read Ephesians 6:14-17. This is the description of what a warrior and warrioress look like in the spiritual realm. We fight spiritually. We behave spiritually. We think spiritually. We respond spiritually. We defend spiritually. We attack spiritually.

3. The piece of armor that holds everything together is the belt. What does the belt represent (verse 14)?

This is what you have been studying for the past five weeks—truth. You have been putting truth in you, building up your spirit, and coming against lies you have believed since you were a little girl. No more lies, sister! Hold on to truth!

4. What assurance does Jesus give His believers in John 14:15-17?

5. According to Ephesians 6:14b, what does the breastplate represent?

I know you already know whose righteousness protects us. Paul got it right when he confessed, "not having a righteousness of my own that comes from the law, but that which is through faith in Christ—the righteousness that comes from God is by faith" (Philippians 3:9). Believe it or not, sometimes the truth of whose righteousness is on us protects us against ourselves. Whew! That hits us in our pride. That is what it is meant to do.

6. Paul warns the church at Corinth against what kind of pride in 1 Corinthians 1:28-31?

Look at 1 Corinthians 1:31 in *The Message*:

"Take a good look, friends, at who you were when you got called into this life. I don't see many of 'the brightest and the best' among you, not many influential, not many from high-society families. Isn't it obvious that God deliberately chose men and women that the culture overlooks and exploits and abuses, chose these 'nobodies' to expose the hollow pretensions of the 'somebodies'? That makes it quite clear that none of you can get by with blowing your own horn before God. Everything that we have—right thinking and right living, a clean slate and a fresh start—comes from God by way of Jesus Christ. That's why we have the saying, 'If you're going to blow a horn, blow a trumpet for God.'"

6. In what way(s) are you tempted to "blow your own horn"?

7. What does the "feet fitted with readiness" represent (Ephesians 6:15)?

161

Peace? Really? Who is kidding who? We are supposed to have peace when the vast army has a surprise attack against us? When the waters are at flood stage? When the wall is bigger and stronger than my puny resources? When the giant has a reputation longer than I have been alive? Or when the work required of me is more than I have the strength for? You may say like Job, "I have no peace, no quietness; I have no rest, but only turmoil" (Job 3:26). How? How is peace possible?

Before Jesus was even on this earth, the prophet Isaiah predicted that through the line of David, One would be born of a virgin who would be given the names "Wonderful Counselor, Mighty God, Everlasting Father, Prince of Peace" (Isaiah 9:6). Jesus was born to fulfill all four of these amazing callings to each of us. Supplying us with peace has already been checked off His "to do list." He is ours. We are His. Peace is ours. Peace is Him.

8. What do you learn about peace from the following verses?

Psalm 29:11

Isaiah 26:3

Isaiah 26:12-13

Ephesians 2:14

Philippians 4:7

2 Thessalonians 3:16

During the worst of the worst, sad situations, painstaking dilemmas, grieving diagnosis, or unspeakable loss, it really is possible to experience peace that cannot be explained. Human tendencies are to freak out and panic, but a warrior and warrioress are ones, who despite the circumstance, will stand in God's peace and have a clear mind in order to make right decisions.

9. Have you or have you known someone that had God's peace even through a trial of some kind? Explain the peace you or the other person experienced.

The Psalmist describes one who wholly trusts in God: "He will have no fear of bad news; his heart is steadfast, trusting in the LORD. His heart is secure, he will have no fear; in the end he looks in triumph on his foes" (Psalm 112:7-8).

Dear Heavenly Father, You are peace. You are my peace even in my thoughts, my responses, my actions, and my attitude. I will be still and know that You are God (Psalm 46:10).

WEEK 6

DAY 3: WITH MY MOUTH

"I will sing of the LORD's great love forever; with my mouth I will make your faithfulness known through all generations."

PSALM 89:1

1. For the sake of repetition, please write Ephesians 6:16 in the space below.

When the flaming arrows are aimed at us, when the flaming arrows are quick, when the flaming arrows send the heat, when the flaming arrows get near, hold up your shield of faith.

2. According to Ephesians 6:16, faith does what to the flaming arrows?

Psalm 140 is full of imagery that easily symbolizes for us the arrows meant "to kill, steal, and destroy" (John 10:10a). The psalmist David wrote of evil men "who devise evil plans in their hearts and stir up war everyday" (Psalm 140:1-2). That evil men also have "the poison of vipers" on their lips, and that men of violence "plan to trip my feet" (Psalm 140: 3-4). He continues that proud men who "have hidden a snare," "spread out the cords of their net" for him (Psalm 140:5). Your very faith pours water on those evil plans, on the poison of the vipers, on the cords of their nets meant to come against you. How does faith do that? I am glad you asked.

3. Read 2 Corinthians 4:13-14. What is the action associated with believing?

4. Of what spirit do we believe and speak?

5. Now read 2 Corinthians 4:17-18. What achieved an eternal glory?

6. What do we not fix our eyes on?

7. On what do we fix our eyes?

8. What is the definition of faith according to Hebrews 11:1?

By faith, we believe even though we may not see any evidence of the outcome in the natural—yet. We are sure of what we hope for because we know the living God we serve. Because we believe we will speak it out as truth. Our words will testify to our beliefs. I can't think of a better appropriation than to speak our faith through speaking and singing praises to our God.

9. When King David was being hunted by his enemies, what does he decide to do according to Psalm 71:14-18, 22-24?

10. According to verse 24, what happened to those who meant him harm?

We have yet to conclude the real-life drama of Jehoshaphat and the people of Judah. Please turn again to 2 Chronicles 20, reading verses 20-26.

11. What were the promises associated with having faith?

12. Who did Jehoshaphat appoint, and what was their literal position in the war?

13. What were the words they sang?

14. What did God do as they sang and praised God?

15. What did the men of Judah find as they looked upon the vast army?

Stormie Omartian in her book, *The Prayer that Changes Everything,* has some powerful words for us in light of this passage of Scripture: "If you are in a place where you need the enemy to get his hands off of you or the life of the people and things you care about, then praise God right now. Confuse the enemy with your worship and destroy his hold on you. Enter into God's presence and tell Him you need Him to fight the battle for you. Praise Him as your Almighty Deliverer and Defender. Say as Jehoshaphat did 'My eyes are upon You, Lord!' Then position yourself in a stance and attitude of worship, and know that God is with you and will put you on a firm foundation."[21]

Stormie is right. Praising God destroys the stronghold. Whether we speak the truths of God's Word and His promises aloud or put some worship music on and declare aloud who our God is. Our words have divine power. The spiritual weapon of praise cuts through unbelief, lies, anger, fear, and strongholds. The spiritual weapon of praise gives back faith, truth, peace, joy, and freedom.

Let's take a look at a New Testament miracle of the same kind. Please read Acts 16:22-40.

16. What were Paul and Silas doing right before the earthquake?

17. Whose chains were released?

18. What was the outcome of the miracle?

19. Who escorted the prisoners out of jail?

20. What part of this miracle fuels your faith?

Go back to 2 Chronicles 20:21. Look again at the song they chose to lead the army in singing. They were not only praising, but giving thanks.

21. For what do you think they were giving God thanks?

Yes, they were singing of His love, but what else? They didn't know the outcome at the end of the day. For all they knew they were singing their own funeral song. They hadn't gotten a heads up that the enemies who came to attack them ended up killing one another. They only knew what happened when they saw with their own eyes the dead bodies on the battlefield. They didn't have to kill one person. They got the job of taking the plunder! They were most likely giving thanks ahead of time for what they believed God would do for them.

22. Can you do that today? Can you give thanks to God ahead of time no matter the outcome? No matter what, Fierce Warrioress, His love endures. Romans 8:38-39 says, "For I am convinced that neither death nor life, neither angels nor demons, neither the present nor the future, nor any powers, neither height nor depth, nor anything else in all creation, will be able to separate us from the love of God that is in Christ Jesus our Lord."

Consider memorizing these verses: "Praise the LORD, O my soul; all my inmost being, praise his holy name. Praise the LORD, my soul, and forget not all his benefits—who forgives all your sins and heals all your diseases, who redeems your life from the pit and crowns you with love and compassion, who satisfies your desires with good things so that your youth is renewed like the eagle's" (Psalm 103:1-5).

Time to add another tactic to your shield. Please write: "I will praise my Lord."

Dear Heavenly Father, You are worthy of my praise. I open my mouth and speak and sing Your praises. I give You thanks for all You are, all You have been, and all You will be.

DAY 4: THE HOLY SCRIPTURES

"And how from infancy you have known the Holy Scriptures, which are able to make you wise for salvation through faith in Christ Jesus."

2 TIMOTHY 3:15

Having known the Scriptures from infancy does not equal a boring life. If there is anything God or the Bible or the Christian life equals, it is adventure, intrigue, callings, and purpose. Talk about living on the edge; God can take us places we never fathomed! I hope that even in your time spent in this Bible study has proven not to be boring but served as an appetizer to the deeper things of God. I do hope you continue your search for biblical answers to any and all questions you have this side of heaven.

1. Please read Ephesians 6:17-18. From verse 17, what two pieces are we to "take"? What do each represent?

Obviously, a helmet protects one's head from all types of artillery. Your head holds a very vital organ that affects you physically, emotionally, intellectually, and spiritually—your mind. I think this is Paul's way of stating: "Remember the Lord."

2. According to Acts 4:10-12, where is salvation found?

3. According to 1 Corinthians 1:18, the message of the cross is what?

Our power lies not in our own knowledge, not in our own wisdom, not in our own understanding, but only in the One who has saved us. Our goal is not for people to ooh and aww over us and what we have overcome and conquered, but to be a "demonstration of the Spirit's power" (1 Corinthians 2:4).

4. What do we learn from 2 Timothy 3:16-17 about God's Holy Word and its uses?

5. For what does the Word of God equip you?

No doubt Jesus was equipped. We have yet to examine the Scriptures of when Jesus was tempted. I cannot think of a more opportune time than now. Please read Matthew 4:1-11.

6. Who led Jesus into the desert?

7. Who tempted Jesus?

8. What did Jesus use to combat the devil?

9. Who left Jesus and who came to Jesus after He resisted Satan's ploys?

Jesus modeled for us what to do when the enemy tempts us by speaking Scripture to combat the twisted schemes of the devil. Jesus stood firm in what He knew to be the truth. God's truth trumps Satan's "truth" every single time. The spiritual weapon of speaking God's Word cuts through demonic activity, pride, narcissism, lust, carnality, self-righteousness, and self-exaltation.

The spiritual weapon of speaking God's Word gives back truth, humility, Christlikeness, holiness, and power to overcome the evil one.

The helmet of salvation and the sword of the Spirit identifies a man or woman of war of belonging to the Lord's army. Both give proof as to whose side you are fighting for—kingdom of light against the kingdom of darkness. "There is no neutral ground in the spiritual battle between the forces of God and the forces of the devil."[22]

10. As we know, with great privileges come great responsibilities. Last, but certainly not in the least, what are we responsible to do as we fight spiritual battles in Ephesians 6:18?

11. We should pray when and how often?

12. How actively and often do you pray?

13. Are there certain occasions or time you pray the most?

14. Are there certain occasions or times you tend to pray the least?

15. Do you regularly pray with a group?

16. Do you ask for prayer? If so, for what reasons? If not, what hinders you?

17. First Peter 1:7 tells us that "all kinds of trials" have come so that we have an opportunity to prove our faith to God, ourselves, and those around us, and that it results in what three things?

Once again we recognize that faith produces praise to God. I can guarantee that the person—who has suffered through the various trials and came out on the other side with an authentic faith in God—is one who prayed "all kinds of prayers and requests."

Sometimes our approach to God (I know I am guilty of this) is one like the father of a demon-possessed boy who looked Jesus in the face and said, "But *if you can* do anything, take pity on us and help us" (Mark 9:21b, italics added for emphasis). We may close our eyes or get on our knees and ask God to do a work in our lives or the life of a loved one, but deep down we doubt if God will come through for us. Jesus basically replied to the father that of course *He can* do something. It seems Jesus held back a little and really wanted to give the man a piece of His mind, as if to say, "You idiot; don't you know with whom you are speaking?" The boy's father wisely responded to Jesus, "I do believe; help me overcome unbelief!" (Mark 9:24). Then Jesus rebuked the deaf and mute spirit off of the boy and lifted the boy to his feet. The boy's father witnessed a miracle in the presence of Jesus.

"Now to him who is able to do immeasurably more than all we ask or imagine, according to his power that is at work within us, to him be glory in the church and in Christ Jesus throughout all generations, for ever and ever! Amen" (Ephesians 3:20-21).

Let's add another tactic to your shield. On your eleventh blank please write: "I will speak God's Word."

Dear Heavenly Father, help my unbelief! I believe You are able to hear my prayer and to do miracles in my life and in the lives of those for whom I pray. May You be glorified through me and to all my descendants after me.

Day 5: Be Alert

"With this in mind, be alert and always keep on praying for all the Lord's people."

Ephesians 6:18

*I*f there is one thing I pray you will come away with after participating in *Fierce Warrioress* is that you are not afraid of Satan or his demons knowing that "the one who is in you is greater than the one who is in the world" (1 John 4:4).

1. Why do you not need to fear our spiritual enemy?

2. How does remembering the Lord downplay any reaction to panic or to give in to paranoia?

3. As you fight against the enemy, what is your battle plan?

Another thing I hope you take away from this study is that you know you really are a royal princess in Christ, you really are an heiress to the Kingdom of God, and that you really are a fierce Warrioress ready to do battle for your own heart and for the spiritual well-being of those you care about. Just because we are women does not excuse us to a life of glamour and sitting around looking pretty as if it is all about having our pictures taken. It doesn't excuse us to a life of letting others, especially a man, do all the work. It doesn't excuse us to a life of what we can only see in the natural. Our wardrobe consists far much more than the clothes hanging in our closets. God desires we put on His heavenly armor to march out of our corridors confident of His charge over us to display His glory through our callings. There are battles to be fought, souls to be saved, hearts to be mended, captives to be freed, and sorrow to be turned to joy.

"Jesus came through for us before we were even born. He fought for us before we even knew we needed him. He came, he died, he rose again *for us.* He was given all the authority in heaven and on earth *for us* (Ephesians 1:22). He has won the decisive victory against our Enemy. *But we must apply it.* Christianity is not a passive religion. It is an invasion of a Kingdom. We who are on the Lord's side must wield his victory. We must learn to enforce it. Women need to grow as warriors because we, too, were created to reign. God said of Eve as well as Adam, 'and let them rule' (Genesis 1:26). And one day we will rule again (Matthew 25:21, Revelation 22:5). God allows spiritual warfare and uses it in our lives for our good. It is how we learn to grow in exercising our God-given spiritual authority as women."[23]

The spiritual weapon of prayer does more in our pursuit of victory than we will ever truly know until we see it all unveiled in heaven. I am convinced that our prayers in the Spirit do more damage to the kingdom of darkness and allow the kingdom of light more ammunition than our natural eyes are capable of viewing.

The opposite is truer than we want to give it credit. Our spoken words can align with the evil realm. "The tongue is also a fire, a world of evil among the parts of the body. It corrupts the whole person, sets the whole course of his life on fire, and itself is on fire by hell" (James 3:6).

4. What are examples of how our tongues can contaminate our bodies?

Let's turn our attention to a fascinating portion of Scripture involving prayer, demonic activity, and angelic beings. Daniel was one of the "cream of the crop" of Israelites chosen to be taken into Babylonian captivity to be educated on the ways of the Babylonians (Daniel 1:3-4). On behalf of God's people, who were also taken into captivity later, Daniel interceded through "prayer and petition, in fasting, and in sackcloth and ashes" (Daniel 9:3). His prayer is highly interesting. If you want to read it in full you may, or just read verses 17-27.

5. What do you think Daniel's tone (attitude) reveals?

6. Who came in "swift flight" while Daniel was still speaking, praying, and confessing?

Gabriel, whose name means "mighty man of God," is one of the only two angels in the Bible mentioned by name. The other angel is Michael.

7. When was the answer to Daniel's prayer?

8. This is not an isolated case of God answering a prayer the moment someone lifted up their words to Him. From the following verses record what the Bible says about prayer.

Isaiah 30:19

Matthew 6:8

Matthew 7:7-12

Years later, Daniel was given a revelation and the meaning of it came to him in a vision (Daniel 10:1). Please read of his vision in Daniel 10:4-14.

9. What does the angelic being specifically ask Daniel to do?

Exactly! He advised him to consider carefully his words and to "stand up" and to "not be afraid." This is the position of a warrior and warrioress.

10. When was Daniel's praying first heard?

11. Why didn't the angel get to come sooner?

12. Who came to help this angel and what was his title?

This is another one of those pull back the curtain moments of the heavenlies. Angels and demons really do war against one another because of us. We would be amazed if we saw all the warring in the heavenlies because of the prayers of all kinds from godly men and women lifting their voices to God.

Let's conclude by reading a New Testament account of answered prayer where the prayer warriors got a surprise knock at the door. Please read Acts 12:1-19.

James, one of the apostles who spread the good news of salvation through Jesus Christ, the Messiah, had just been put to death (Acts 5:29-33). Now another powerhouse apostle, Peter, was in prison under the same charges.

13. Who was praying for Peter?

14. How did God answer their prayers?

While they were still gathered in prayer, God sent an angel to rescue Peter from prison. Peter then showed up at the doorstep of the home where the church was praying. It is almost a comical scene . . . until we realize we can react the exact way.

15. What was the response of the church?

We can be like the first church; we can pray but not believe He will come through for us. The reality of Peter being killed like James probably prevailed the minds of the church. But God. But God "sent his angel and rescued me from Herod's clutches and from everything the Jewish people were hoping would happen" (Acts 12:11).

As you pray for deliverance, healing, repentance, reconciliation, preservation, or in whatever you need God alone to do, there is no need to fear. You are not alone. When you praise God and pray to Him you are standing on the battlefield against a foe that only seems stronger than yourself. Fierce Warrioress, you are standing on holy ground. You are smack dab in the presence of the Almighty God. Take refuge under His wings. He is fighting for you! Stand firm!

For our last, but certainly not in the least, battle plan tactic of spiritual warfare, please write: "I will pray to my Lord."

Dear Heavenly Father, "The LORD is my light and my salvation—whom shall I fear? The LORD is the stronghold of my life—of whom shall I be afraid? When the wicked advance against me to devour me, it is my enemies and my foes who will stumble and fall. Though an army besiege me, my heart will not fear; though war break out against me, even then will I be confident" (Psalm 27:1-3).

Recommended Reading from the Author:

Lord is it Warfare; Teach Me to Stand by Kay Arthur

Believing God by Beth Moore

Breaking Free by Beth Moore

Spiritual Warfare: The Battle for God's Glory by Jerry Rankin

Bondage Breaker by Neil T. Anderson

The Prayer That Changes Everything by Stormie OMartian

Captivity by John and Stasi Eldredge

Piercing the Darkness by Frank Peretti

This Present Darkness by Frank Peretti

Screwtape Letters by C.S. Lewis

ENDNOTES

[1]Strong, James. *The Exhaustive Concordance of the Bible: Showing Every Word of the English Revised Version and the Authorized or King James Version and Every Occurrence of Each Word in Regular Order, Together with Dictionaries of the Original Hebrew Old Testament and the Greek New Testament.* Nashville, TN: Broadman & Holman, n.d. Print

[2]Kay Arthur, *LORD, Is It Warfare? Teach Me to Stand,* WaterBrook Press, Colorado Springs, CO: 1991, p. 185.

[3]Youngblood, Ronald F., F. F. Bruce, and R. K. Harrison. *Nelson's New Illustrated Bible Dictionary,* Nashville, TN: Thomas Nelson, 1995. 1302. Print.

[4]"Lord, Kinsmen Redeemer, How Can Satan Be Defeated?" *Lord, Is It Warfare?: Teach Me to Stand.* Portland, OR: Multnomah, 1991. 179. Print.

[5]Pearcey, Nancy. "Chapter 13." *Total Truth: Liberating Christianity from Its Cultural Captivity.* Wheaton, IL: Crossway, 2004. 357. Print.

[6]Pearcey, Nancy. "Chapter 2." *Total Truth: Liberating Christianity from Its Cultural Captivity.* Wheaton, IL: Crossway, 2004. 90-91. Print.

[7]Alcorn, Randy C. "Chapter 10." *Heaven.* Wheaton, IL: Tyndale House, 2004. 103. Print.

[8]@BethMooreLPM, July 25, 2013.

[9]Walvoord, John F., and Roy B. Zuck. "1 John." *The Bible Knowledge Commentary: An Exposition of the Scriptures.* Wheaton, IL: Victor, 1983. 900-01. Print.

[10]Strong, James. *The Exhaustive Concordance of the Bible: Showing Every Word of the English Revised Version and the Authorized or King James Version and Every Occurrence of Each Word in Regular Order, Together with Dictionaries of the Original Hebrew Old Testament and the Greek New Testament.* Nashville, TN: Broadman & Holman. 9. Print.

[11]Yancey, 41.

[12]Warren, Richard. *The Purpose-driven Life: What on Earth Am I Here For?* Grand Rapids, MI: Zondervan, 2002. 186. Print.

[13]Yancey, Philip. *Rumors of Another World: What on Earth Are We Missing?* Grand Rapids, MI: Zondervan, 2003. 50. Print.

[14]Green, Dr. Charles E. *The Lord Heard My Cry,* Franklin, TN: Providence House Publishers, 1995.

[15]Arthur, Kay. "Lord, Satan's Roaring—Need I Fear?" *Lord, Is It Warfare?: Teach Me to Stand.* Portland, OR: Multnomah, 1991. 51. Print.

[16]Arthur, Kay. "Lord, the Enemy's Accusing Me!" *Lord, Is It Warfare?: Teach Me to Stand.* Portland, OR: Multnomah, 1991. 114. Print.

[17]"Supernatural." *Dictionary.com*. Dictionary.com, n.d. Web. 09 Mar. 2014.

[18]Arthur, Kay. "Lord, Kinsman Redeemer, How Can Satan be Defeated?" *Lord, Is It Warfare? Teach Me to Stand*. Portland, OR: Multnomah, 1991. 168. Print.

[19]Moore, Pamela Rosewell. "In the Power of the Holy Spirit." *Life Lessons from the Hiding Place: Discovering the Heart of Corrie Ten Boom*. Grand Rapids, MI: Chosen, 2004. 138. Print.

[20]Batterson, Mark. "The Speed of Prayer." *The Circle Maker: Praying Circles around Your Biggest Dreams and Greatest Fears*. Grand Rapids, MI: Zondervan, 2011. 165-66. Print.

[21]Omartian, Stormie. "When I Am Attacked by the Enemy." *The Prayer That Changes Everything*. Eugene, OR: Harvest House, 2004. 291. Print.

[22]Pearcey, Nancy. "What's Next? Living it Out." *Total Truth: Liberating Christianity from Its Cultural Captivity*. Wheaton, IL: Crossway, 2004. 360. Print.

[23]Eldredge, John and Stasi, "Warrior Princess," *Captivating*, Nashville, TN: Thomas Nelson Publishers, 2005. 196.

My Spiritual Battle Plan

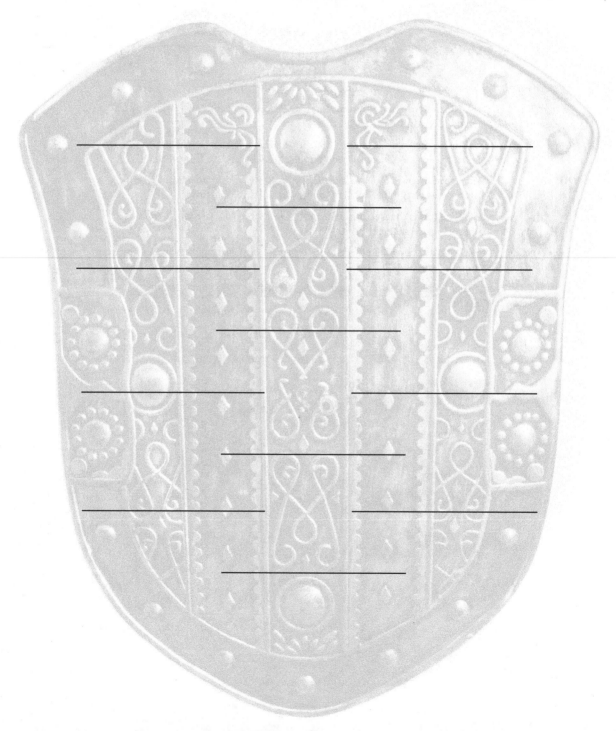